The Trial of John Brown

Radical Abolitionist

FAMOUS TRIALS

Titles in the Famous Trials series include:

The Trial of John Brown

Radical Abolitionist

by James Tackach

FAMOUS TRIALS

Lucent Books, P.O. Box 289011, San Diego, CA 92198-9011

Library of Congress Cataloging-in-Publication Data

Tackach, James.
 The trial of John Brown / by James Tackach.
  p. cm. — (Famous trials)
 Includes bibliographical references and index.
 Summary: Focuses on the trial of the abolitionist who was hanged for treason and murder following his attempt to capture a military arsenal and arm the slaves for revolt.
 ISBN 1-56006-468-4 (lib.)
 1. Brown, John, 1800–1859—Juvenile literature. 2. Brown, John, 1800–1859—Trials, litigation, etc.—Juvenile literature. 3. Trials (Treason)—West Virginia—Charles Town—Juvenile literature. 4. Trials (Murder)—West Virginia—Charles Town—Juvenile literature. 5. Abolitionists—United States—Biography—Juvenile literature. 6. Antislavery movements—United States—History—19th century—Juvenile literature. [1. Brown, John, 1800–1859—Trials, litigation, etc. 2. Trials (Treason). 3. Trials (Murder). 4. Abolitionists. 5. Antislavery movements.] I. Title. II. Series.
E451.T117   1998
973.6'8'092
[B]—DC21   97-39780
                                                        CIP
                                                        AC

Copyright © 1998 by Lucent Books, Inc.
P.O. Box 289011
San Diego, CA 92198-9011
Printed in the U.S.A.

Table of Contents

Foreword

"The law is not an end in and of itself, nor does it provide ends. It is preeminently a means to serve what we think is right."

William J. Brennan Jr.

THE CONCEPT OF JUSTICE AND THE RULE OF LAW are hallmarks of Western civilization, manifested perhaps most visibly in widely famous and dramatic court trials. These trials include such important and memorable personages as the ancient Greek philosopher Socrates, who was accused and convicted of corrupting the minds of his society's youth in 399 B.C.; the French maiden and military leader Joan of Arc, accused and convicted of heresy against the church in 1431; to former football star O.J. Simpson, acquitted of double murder in 1995. These and other well-known and controversial trials constitute the most public, and therefore most familiar, demonstrations of a Western legal tradition that dates back through the ages. Although no one is certain when the first law code appeared or when the first formal court trials were held, Babylonian ruler Hammurabi introduced the first known law code in about 1760 B.C. It remains unclear how this code was administered, and no records of specific trials have survived. What is clear, however, is that humans have always sought to govern behavior and define actions in terms of law.

Almost all societies have made laws and prosecuted people for going against those laws, but the question of which behaviors to sanction and which to censure has always been controversial and remains in flux. Some, such as Roman orator and legislator Cicero, argue that laws are simply applications of universal standards. Cicero believed that humanity would agree on what constituted illegal behavior and that human laws were a mere extension of natural laws. "True law is right reason in agreement with nature," he wrote, world-wide in scope, unchanging, everlasting. . . . We may not oppose or alter that law, we cannot abolish it, we cannot be freed from its obligations by any legislature. . . . This [natural] law does not differ for Rome and for Athens, for the present and for the future. . . . It is and will be valid for all nations and all times.

Cicero's rather optimistic view has been contradicted throughout history, however. For every law made to preserve harmony and set universal standards of behavior, another has been born of fear, prejudice, greed, desire for power, and a host of other motives. History is replete with individuals defying and fighting to change such laws—and even to topple governments that dictate such laws. Abolitionists fought against slavery, civil rights leaders fought for equal rights, millions throughout the world have fought for independence—these constitute a minimum of reasons for which people have sought to overturn laws that they believed to be wrong or unjust. In opposition to Cicero, then, many others, such as eighteenth-century English poet and philosopher William Godwin, believe humans must be constantly vigilant against bad laws. As Godwin said in 1793:

Laws we sometimes call the wisdom of our ancestors. But this is a strange imposition. It was as frequently the dictate of their passion, of timidity, jealousy, a monopolizing spirit, and a lust of power that knew no bounds. Are we not obliged perpetually to renew and remodel this misnamed wisdom of our ancestors? To correct it by a detection of their ignorance, and a censure of their intolerance?

Lucent Books' *Famous Trials* series showcases trials that exemplify both society's praiseworthy condemnation of universally unacceptable behavior, and its misguided persecution of individuals based on fear and ignorance, as well as trials that leave open the question of whether justice has been done. Each volume begins by setting the scene and providing a historical context to show how society's mores influence the trial process and the verdict.

Each book goes on to present a detailed and lively account of the trial, including liberal use of primary source material such as direct testimony, lawyers' summations, and contemporary and modern commentary. In addition, sidebars throughout the text create a broader context by presenting illuminating details about important points of law, information on key personalities, and important distinctions related to civil, federal, and criminal procedures. Thus, all of the primary and secondary source material included in both the text and the sidebars demonstrates to readers the sources and methods historians use to derive information and conclusions about such events.

Lastly, each *Famous Trials* volume includes one or more of the following comprehensive tools that motivate readers to pursue further reading and research. A timeline allows readers to see the scope of the trial at a glance, annotated bibliographies provide both sources for further research and a thorough list of works consulted, a glossary helps students with unfamiliar words and concepts, and a comprehensive index permits quick scanning of the book as a whole.

The insight of Oliver Wendell Holmes Jr., distinguished Supreme Court justice, exemplifies the theme of the *Famous Trials* series. Taken from *The Common Law*, published in 1881, Holmes remarked: "The life of the law has not been logic, it has been experience." That "experience" consists mainly in how laws are applied in society and challenged in the courts, a process resulting in differing outcomes from one generation to the next. Thus, the *Famous Trials* series encourages readers to examine trials within a broader historical and social context.

Introduction

John Brown: Traitor or Martyr?

T HE PAGES OF AMERICAN HISTORY BOOKS record the deeds of many individuals whose lives have provoked continual controversy. Thomas Jefferson, for example, is admired by many for composing the stirring words of the Declaration of Independence—a document that clearly asserts that "all men are created equal"—yet he is condemned by others as an owner of slaves. General Robert E. Lee is denounced by some as a traitor who waged a bloody civil war that almost divided the United States into two separate countries, but he is also praised by many as a superb military commander who fought gallantly in defense of his home state of Virginia and who accepted defeat on the battlefield with grace and dignity. President Lyndon Johnson's ardent defenders hail his Great Society programs, which attempted to abolish poverty in America, and his civil rights initiatives, which strove to bring justice and equality to African Americans. Johnson's detractors, however, criticize him as the president who badly blundered by escalating U.S. involvement in the Vietnam War.

Students of American history will encounter no figure more controversial than the man whose trial is the focus of this book. On December 2, 1859, John Brown, after a trial that captivated the nation, was hanged for two of the most serious crimes that an American citizen can commit: treason and murder. Nonetheless, on the

day of his death, church bells tolled for a fallen martyr; and ministers, politicians, and famous authors delivered stirring speeches and
eulogies that honored a saintly man and national hero.

Brown was sentenced to death for attempting to capture the
U.S. military arsenal at Harpers Ferry, Virginia, after which he
intended to arm the slaves who lived and labored on nearby plantations so that they could revolt against their masters and gain their
freedom. Brown had hoped that the slave rebellion at Harpers Ferry
would spread, first through Virginia and nearby Maryland and then
throughout the entire South. Brown firmly believed that American
slavery was both a sin against God and a violation of the sacred principles articulated by Jefferson in the Declaration of Independence;
and Brown had gradually come to the conclusion that only a violent
revolution undertaken by the slaves themselves against their masters could rid America of the heinous institution of slavery.

Defended and Denounced

Although his crimes were most serious, John Brown, and his supporters, defended his actions by asserting that he had performed
them for a noble and even holy purpose. Throughout the South,
however, Brown was denounced as an agent of Satan whose goal
was either to destroy the region's social and economic order or to
lead the United States into civil war over the issue of slavery.
Even many Americans who believed that slavery ought to be
abolished censured Brown as a man who violently and destruc-
tively took the law into his own hands instead of working
through proper legal channels to achieve his goal of curtailing or
eliminating American slavery.

When Brown's trial commenced on October 25, 1859, American slavery itself was put on trial. Would the jury condemn Brown
for trying to destroy slavery and thereby assert the right of Southern slave owners to retain their human property? Or would Brown
be exonerated, suggesting that slavery was an evil that Brown had
justly attempted to destroy? The entire nation—North and South,
slave owners and passionate abolitionists—waited for news of the
verdict from the county courthouse in Charles Town, Virginia,
where the week-long trial of John Brown took place.

John Brown fired the first shots of the Civil War during his standoff at Harpers Ferry, Virginia, where he hoped to instigate a slave rebellion.

Regardless of how they stood on the issue of slavery, however, most Americans living at and after the time of John Brown's trial would agree on one point: Brown's actions at Harpers Ferry were the first shots fired in the Civil War. The war actually began sixteen months after Brown's execution, but his effort to liberate the slaves and his subsequent trial and execution had further divided an already divided nation, setting the United States on a deadly and disastrous course. As historian and Brown biographer Stephen B. Oates asserts, "His raid and public execution had set in motion a spiral of accusations and counteraccusations between Northerners and Southerners that spun the nation inexorably toward civil war."

Chapter 1

The Man and
His Cause

T HE MAN WHOSE TRIAL FORESHADOWED the Civil War had
humble beginnings. John Brown's father, Owen, was a tan-
ner who labored hard merely to keep his family out of poverty.
Owen's first wife, Ruth, John's mother, was the daughter of a
Congregational minister. The Browns hailed from Connecticut;
and in 1799, the year before John's birth, they purchased a mod-
est farm in the small town of Torrington in the northwestern part
of the state. John was the Browns' third of six children, including an orphan boy whom the family adopted and raised. In 1805
Owen Brown, barely able to support his family on his tanning
business and frustrated with Connecticut's rocky soil, moved his
family west to Ohio, where young John grew to adulthood.

In many ways, John Brown's boyhood was ordinary, and the
Browns' lives were typical of an early-nineteenth-century American farm family. They toiled hard in the fields and prayed hard
that the earth would provide them with enough food to nourish
the family. But John Brown did not grow to adulthood during
ordinary times. In 1800 the United States was still a very young
nation, and as the country and John Brown matured, Americans
began undertaking a sixty-year debate on the issue of slavery, a
debate that would eventually energize Brown and plunge the
United States into a bloody and costly civil war.

Owen Brown was a religious man who taught his children to
fear God and to avoid sin. Early in his life, a minister Owen

worked for told him that slavery was a grievous sin against God, that all people, black slaves included, were children of God who deserved love and respect; and Owen later pressed these beliefs upon his family. He taught his children that God would eventually punish America severely for tolerating slavery, and young John took this lesson to heart.

When John was about twelve or thirteen years old, an experience that he would long remember validated his father's teachings about slavery. Even at this young age, John had been assigned the job of driving his father's cattle for sale to an army outpost a hundred miles away in the Michigan territory. Once, while on one of these drives, John lodged at the home of a man who owned a slave boy about John's age. The boy was poorly clothed and malnourished. Worse, one day John observed the man beating his slave severely with a fire shovel when the boy had performed poorly at some task. John painfully remembered the boy's screams as he accepted his awful punishment.

TO BE SOLD on board the Ship *Bance-Island*, on tuesday the 6th of *May* next, at *Ashley-Ferry*; a choice cargo of about 250 fine healthy

NEGROES,

just arrived from the Windward & Rice Coast. —The utmost care has already been taken, and shall be continued, to keep them free from the least danger of being infected with the SMALL-POX, no boat having been on board, and all other communication with people from *Charles-Town* prevented.

Austin, Laurens, & Appleby.

N. B. Full one Half of the above Negroes have had the SMALL-POX in their own Country.

(Above) An advertisement for a slave auction and (left) the mangled, scarred back of a slave testify to a time in America's history when the owning and selling of blacks was permitted.

JOHN BROWN'S RELIGION

John Brown was raised according to the principles of the Calvinist faith. Calvinists embraced the religious creed of John Calvin, a sixteenth-century religious reformer who was one of the leaders in the Protestant Reformation. The English Puritans who immigrated to Massachusetts Bay Colony during the seventeenth and eighteenth centuries were Calvinists, and their faith was still widely practiced at the beginning of the nineteenth century, particularly in New England.

Calvinists believed that human beings were essentially evil and that most would be condemned by God to everlasting punishment in hell because of their sins. God would select only a few individual souls for redemption.

Above all, Calvinists believed in a powerful and vengeful God who would severely punish those who disobeyed his commandments, an Old Testament God filled with anger and fury at the unholy lives of most human beings. According to the Calvinists, God played a very direct role in the everyday affairs of humankind, particularly when his anger was provoked by widespread sin. An epidemic of illness or a long drought that ruined crops would be viewed as a punishment sent by God against a community that had sinned extensively.

John Brown had been taught by his father that slavery was a serious sin against God and that someday God would exact a fierce punishment on America for allowing slavery to exist. Brown later came to see himself as an instrument in the hands of God who was chosen to administer God's punishment against the slaveholders of the South.

John Brown was not alone in his belief that God would inflict a strict punishment upon the United States for its tolerance of slavery. Many abolitionists held the same beliefs. In 1829 David Walker, an African American abolitionist, dramatically warned his readers in *Walker's Appeal:* "I tell you Americans! that unless you alter your course, *you* and your country are gone!!!!! For God Almighty will tear up the very face of the earth!!!!!" At the end of *Uncle Tom's Cabin*, Harriet Beecher Stowe similarly warned her readers that "both North and South have been guilty before God," and that the injustices and cruelties like those inflicted by American slavery "shall bring on nations the wrath of Almighty God!"

Many abolitionists would later see the Civil War as God's vengeance against the United States for the sin of slavery. Near the end of the war, President Abraham Lincoln, in his Second Inaugural Address, eloquently articulated that sentiment when he identified American slavery as an offense that God "now wills to remove, and that He gives to both North and South this terrible war as the woe due to those by whom the offense came."

From that moment on, John Brown detested slavery, judging it as his father judged it—a grievous sin against God. He vowed that he would work to free individual slaves and eliminate slavery from his country. Living in the free state of Ohio, the Browns sometimes encountered runaway slaves who had crossed the Ohio River from plantations in the South in quest of freedom in one of the states of the North or in Canada, and several times the family hid and assisted the escapees. Both John and his father believed that it was their Christian duty to help any slave escape to freedom.

On a Course Toward War

As John Brown grew to adulthood and confronted the issue of slavery, his country, too, debated the morality and necessity of this peculiar institution. At the opening of the nineteenth century, Americans had basically struck an unstable compromise on the issue of slavery: It would remain legal in the South but be prohibited in the North, and it would not be allowed to spread to any new territories acquired by the United States.

That fragile agreement was threatened when the territory of Missouri applied for statehood in 1819. At the time, the United States comprised twenty-two states, eleven slave states and eleven free states. Adding Missouri as either a slave or free state would upset the balance between slave and free states and would allow the elected representatives of one side to achieve a majority in the U.S. Senate. After bitter debate on the Missouri question, Congress struck a compromise, known as the Missouri Compromise or the Compromise of 1820. Missouri would be admitted to the Union as a slave state and Maine would be admitted as a free state, maintaining the balance between slave and free states. Also, slavery would be outlawed in any U.S. territories north of latitude 36°30'.

The Missouri Compromise succeeded in diffusing tensions between the North and South for a time. But neither side was truly happy with the agreement. The North had hoped that slavery would be confined to the places where it already existed and would not be allowed to spread into any U.S. territories. The

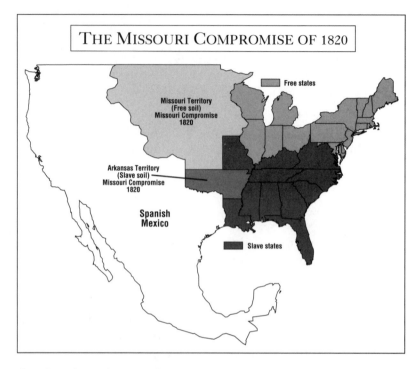

South objected to the federal government's establishment of an arbitrary line of latitude above which slavery could not exist; Southerners believed that each individual state, not the federal government, should decide whether to allow slavery within its borders. In retirement at his Virginia estate, Thomas Jefferson warned that the line of latitude would become a barrier that would further divide the United States into Northern and Southern, anti-slavery and proslavery spheres, thereby hastening the day when the United States would be split into two separate countries.

A Nation Divided

History would prove Jefferson's analysis correct. During the next ten years, proslavery Southerners became more vocal in their defense of slavery, while the number of Americans who demanded an immediate abolishment of slavery gradually grew. Before 1820 the number of abolitionists in the United States was small, and they were judged by many to be extremists or even fanatics. But as the abolitionist forces grew, their message reverberated throughout the country. On January 1, 1831, William Lloyd Garrison, an eloquent abolitionist from Massachusetts, began publishing an antislavery newspaper titled *The Liberator.* In the first issue, Garrison warned slave owners that if slavery was not soon abolished in the United States, the slaves would violently rebel against their masters and bathe the South in blood.

Eight months later Nat Turner, a slave preacher bonded to a Virginia plantation, launched a twelve-hour rebellion with several other slaves that took the lives of sixty plantation owners and their families. Turner was captured and hanged for his offense, but Southerners found little comfort or satisfaction in his execution. The defenders of slavery maintained that Turner had been inspired and supported by abolitionists like Garrison and his followers. Garrison responded by forming the American Anti-Slavery Society, which demanded immediate emancipation of all American slaves, a belief that an increasing number of Northerners came to embrace during the 1830s.

In 1841 Garrison met an escaped slave from Maryland named Frederick Douglass. A self-taught reader and writer, Douglass became one of Garrison's most eloquent spokesmen. His speeches on the evils of slavery captivated audiences, and his first autobiography, *Narrative of the Life of Frederick Douglass, an American Slave*, published in 1845, was the first slave autobiography to be widely distributed and read. Douglass's book drew thousands of sympathetic readers to the abolitionist cause.

Frederick Douglass's widely distributed autobiography, published in 1845, helped the abolitionist cause.

The Compromise of 1850

During the 1840s tensions between the North and South esca-
lated, though both sides prudently avoided a confrontation to
provoke the crisis that would permanently split the nation in two
or lead it into a civil war. In the late 1840s, however, another crisis arose that almost brought the North and South to the brink of
war. As a result of the Mexican War, waged from 1846 through
1848, the United States acquired territory comprising New Mexico and California, and Congress began debating whether slavery
should be allowed in these new territories. The debate was bitter. Many senators and representatives from the Northern states
opposed any extension of slavery, while the elected officials of
the South opposed any restriction imposed on slavery by the
federal government as an intrusion on states' rights. Again, however, a crisis was avoided when three distinguished senators,
Henry Clay of Kentucky, Daniel Webster of Massachusetts, and
Stephen Douglas of Illinois, forged a compromise known as the
Compromise of 1850.

The agreement had four main stipulations. First, California
was admitted to the United States as a free state. Second, the
Utah and New Mexico territories were established, with the
question of slavery to be determined by a vote of the inhabitants

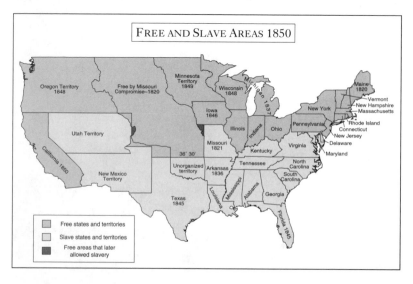

of each territory. Third, the trading and selling of slaves in Washington, D.C., was outlawed. And fourth, a strict fugitive slave law was passed, enabling slave owners to recover runaway slaves more easily than before.

The Compromise of 1850 succeeded in postponing a civil war between the North and South, but both sides found something distasteful about the pact. The South opposed the admission of a free state without the simultaneous admission of a slave state; now the Union would comprise sixteen free states and only fifteen slave states. Northern abolitionists found the new Fugitive Slave Law particularly distasteful.

The law called for the appointment of federal commissioners to seek and apprehend runaway slaves. These commissioners, who were paid ten dollars for each runaway they returned to his or her master, could force citizens to form posses to catch the escapees. Individuals identified as runaway slaves and captured could be returned to their alleged owners without the benefit of a jury trial. Northerners deeply resented that they could be compelled to help arrest a runaway slave in a free state, where slavery itself was prohibited by law. Many abolitionists publicly denounced the law and announced that they would continue to assist escaped slaves who wished to immigrate to Canada, where the Fugitive Slave Law did not apply.

In 1851 one Northern woman who was outraged by the Fugitive Slave Law began writing a series of fictional episodes focusing on a Kentucky slave named Uncle Tom for a weekly abolitionist newspaper titled *National Era*. The author, Harriet Beecher Stowe, the daughter and wife of abolitionist ministers, contributed an episode almost every week, and the demand for copies of the paper increased dramatically. After Stowe penned the final episode nine months later, she arranged to have her story published in novel form, under the title *Uncle Tom's Cabin, or, Life Among the Lowly*. The book became a best-seller, quickly breaking existing sales records in its first month of publication. *Uncle Tom's Cabin* vividly depicts the horrors of slavery—the hard labor without pay, the beatings of disobedient slaves, the breakup of slave families. Americans who had never before considered

Harriet Beecher Stowe's Uncle Tom's Cabin *is a dramatic story of the horrors of slavery. Stowe's novel convinced many people that slavery was wrong.*

slavery to be immoral wept as they read the tragic story of Stowe's main character, Uncle Tom, and ministers used the novel as the subject of Sunday sermons on the evils of slavery.

The Kansas Crisis

Tensions between North and South increased after the passage of the Compromise of 1850. The next major battle between the two sides concerned the Kansas-Nebraska territory, whose population had been steadily rising as settlers from Missouri and Iowa moved westward. These settlers would soon request that their territory be admitted to the Union as a state, and Congress once again had to consider the question of whether slavery would be allowed or outlawed in this region. Senator Stephen Douglas proposed that Congress divide the territory into two separate territories, Kansas and Nebraska. Douglas, however, did not wish one territory to be free and the other slave. He proposed that the 36°30' latitude line established by the Missouri Compromise be erased and that the citizens of each territory vote to decide whether or not their region should allow slavery. He called this practice of letting the people decide the issue of slavery "popular sovereignty." Southerners embraced the idea because it meant that the federal government could no longer dictate where slavery would be allowed and where it would be outlawed. But Northern abolitionists opposed Douglas's doctrine because it meant that slavery could be further extended to U.S. territories and new states.

Douglas's bill, known as the Kansas-Nebraska Act, was passed into law in May 1854 after bitter debate in both the U.S. Senate and the House of Representatives. Almost immediately after the law was passed, both proslavery and antislavery settlers flooded into Kansas, which would be the first of the two territories to vote on whether slavery would be legal within its borders. Settlers on both sides of the slavery issue came to Kansas with the same goal: to establish themselves as residents and participate in the forthcoming election on the slavery issue. Not surprising, conflicts soon arose between proslavery and antislavery settlers.

John Brown's Mission

John Brown grew to adulthood while his troubled nation confronted the slavery issue. He remained a strong abolitionist. In 1820 he married Dianthe Lusk, a young woman from a religious family with strong abolitionist leanings. During the next twelve years, the Browns had seven children, and John Brown instilled in them the same abolitionist beliefs that he himself embraced.

Life was not easy for the Brown family. Like his father, John Brown tried the tanning business, but he failed at that endeavor. He later tried raising cattle and sheep, but he achieved little success in these enterprises. Worse, illness visited his family frequently. In

(Above) Soon after the Kansas-Nebraska Act, hordes of abolitionists and proslavery supporters moved to Kansas, hoping to influence the upcoming election. (Right) Though shaken by family tragedies, John Brown never wavered in his fight against slavery.

1831 his four-year-old son, Frederick, died. A year later Dianthe, after giving birth to her seventh child, took ill and never recovered. She died, as did the newborn child. Brown, too, was frequently beset by burning fevers that left him sick for weeks at a time.

John Brown viewed these illnesses and his financial misfortunes as trials sent to him by God to test his faith. He remained a devout Christian and refused to give in to despair. Less than a year after Dianthe's death, Brown married Mary Day, his housekeeper's sister, and started a second family. Throughout his life, John Brown fathered twenty children, several of whom died in infancy or childhood.

Even during these difficult times, Brown kept abreast of the remarkable political developments that were occurring in his country, particularly those that concerned the issue of slavery. One incident that roused the feelings of Northern abolitionists had a profound effect on Brown. On November 7, 1837, a proslavery mob from Missouri crossed the Mississippi River into Illinois and raided the office of an abolitionist newspaperman named Elijah Lovejoy and shot him to death. A few days later John Brown and his father attended a church service in Hudson, Ohio, where they were then living, in honor of Lovejoy. The minister delivered a stirring antislavery sermon and denounced the newspaperman's killers, after which Brown called for the congregation's attention, raised his right hand, and swore that he would devote the remainder of his life to the destruction of slavery across the United States. The Brown farm became a stop on the Underground Railroad, the secret route by which escaped slaves could cross the Ohio River into Ohio and find freedom in the North or in Canada.

When the Fugitive Slave Law was passed in 1850, Brown reacted with intense anger. He gathered the score of African Americans whom he had befriended in Ohio for a meeting, pressing them to join his United States League of Gileadites, an organization bearing the name of an Old Testament mountain

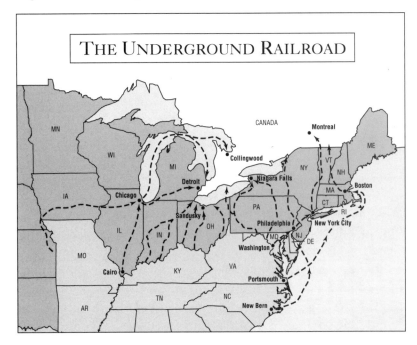

THE UNDERGROUND RAILROAD

from which the Israelites launched a successful attack against their enemies, and dedicated to opposing the Fugitive Slave Law by abetting runaway slaves. Brown even urged the forty-four African Americans who joined his organization to murder slave catchers and commissioners charged with enforcing the new law. Moreover, in his own mind, Brown began forming a plan to gather a small force of abolitionists and travel to the mountains of Alabama, from which they would raid nearby plantations and free the slaves. As Brown began working for the abolitionist cause, he met some of the most prominent antislavery crusaders in the country, including Frederick Douglass.

Brown's Kansas Crusade

Early in 1855, five of John Brown's sons followed thousands of other pioneers who were moving west to Kansas. They were not moving to Kansas specifically to add their names to the list of people who would vote Kansas into the Union as a free state; they left Ohio because a terrible drought had all but ruined their crops, and they had heard excellent reviews about the possibilities of farming in Kansas. The young men settled with their families in eastern Kansas near Pottawatomie Creek.

In the spring of 1855, John Brown Jr. wrote his father a troubling letter. At the time, the elder John Brown was dividing his time between Ohio, where he still had business interests, and North Elba, New York, where he had purchased a farm and sent his wife and younger children. In his letter, John Jr. claimed that thousands of proslavery men "armed to the teeth with Revolvers, Bowie Knives, Rifles & Cannon" were streaming into Kansas intent on evicting antislavery settlers and thereby ensuring that Kansas would be voted into the Union as a slave state. When Brown heard this disturbing news, he determined to venture to Kansas as soon as practical. He left his son Watson in charge of his farm in North Elba and prepared for his journey.

Before heading west, Brown began contacting his prominent friends in the abolitionist movement and soliciting them for funds, which he would use to fight the proslavery forces in Kansas. He obtained some donations and used the money to buy weapons that he would take to Kansas. Included in his cache of weapons were several military broadswords that he would put to use in Kansas. Late in the summer of 1855, Brown, with two of his sons as escorts, headed west to fight against slavery in Kansas.

When Brown arrived in Kansas two months later, the territory was on the verge of civil war. Several clashes had already occurred between the proslavery and antislavery pioneers who had settled in Kansas, and blood had been shed on both sides. During the next six months, the situation deteriorated further. Brown formed his sons and several other antislavery settlers into a militia group that he called the Pottawatomie Rifles. They conducted regular military drills and kept a careful watch on proslavery settlers who settled near Pottawatomie Creek. In late May of 1856, despite Brown's vigilance, proslavery settlers from Missouri attacked and destroyed an antislavery settlement in Lawrence, Kansas. Brown did not want to leave the raid unanswered.

A Night of Terror

On May 23 Brown gathered several of his Pottawatomie Rifles for a secret mission, a swift and violent blow that would avenge the destruction of the Lawrence settlement. They traveled along Pottawatomie Creek until they neared the settlements of the proslavery forces the next day. Having conducted surveillance in the region, Brown knew the farms owned by some of the leaders of the proslavery settlers. At ten o'clock in the evening of May 24, Brown and his followers approached the cabin of Allen Doyle, a proslavery man from Tennessee.

With gun in hand, Brown knocked on Doyle's door. When Doyle asked who was there, Brown replied that he needed to find the home of Allen Wilkinson, another proslavery settler. When Doyle opened the door, Brown and a handful of his armed men stepped inside, Brown announcing to the terrified Doyle that the Northern army had come to pay him a visit. Brown ordered Doyle and his three sons out of the cabin. When Mrs. Doyle begged the intruders not to take her youngest son, Brown allowed the fourteen-year-old boy to stay with his mother in the cabin. Brown led Doyle and his two older sons outside into the night.

About one hundred yards from the Doyle cabin, Brown's two sons, Salmon and Owen, attacked the three Doyles with broadswords. The unarmed men gamely tried to defend themselves and escape, but they were no match for men brandishing weapons. In a few minutes, the Doyles were hacked to death. When the bloody work was finished, Brown drew his pistol, aimed it at the corpse of Allen Doyle, and fired a single shot into the man's forehead.

The Pottawatomie Rifles' work was not yet over. A half mile away was the cabin of Allen Wilkinson. Brown used a similar trick to get himself and his followers into Wilkinson's cabin. Wilkinson asked to be spared because his wife, who was in the

AMERICAN SLAVERY

The first American slaves were a group of Africans kidnapped from their homeland, shipped to America, and sold in Jamestown, Virginia, in 1619. During the next century, slavery spread to all American colonies. Those colonists who owned slaves justified the institution by claiming that the black Africans and their descendants were inferior beings, heathens condemned by God to a life of bondage.

At the time of the American Revolution, more than a half-million African Americans were being held in bondage, mostly in the South. Between 1774 and 1804, all the Northern states outlawed slavery, but it continued to flourish in the South, where many farms and plantations depended on slave labor. In 1793 the invention of the cotton gin—a machine that quickly separated the cotton fiber from its seeds—made cotton a boom crop throughout the South and increased the need for slave labor. By 1860 the American slave population had climbed to almost 4 million.

The Civil War effectively ended American slavery. On January 1, 1863, President Abraham Lincoln implemented the Emancipation Proclamation, a wartime executive order that freed slaves only in the eleven Southern states that had seceded from the Union. The Thirteenth Amendment to the U.S. Constitution, introduced in 1864 and passed in December 1865, several months after the Civil War ended, stated: "Neither slavery nor involuntary servitude, except as a punishment for crime whereof the party shall have been duly convicted, shall exist within the United States, or any place subject to their jurisdiction."

John Brown's companions murder Allen Doyle and his two sons. That same night, they would murder several other proslavery settlers to avenge an attack on an abolitionist settlement.

cabin, was ill with measles and needed someone to care for her. Brown ignored Wilkinson's plea and ordered him outside. A hundred yards from the cabin, two of Brown's recruits fell upon Wilkinson and delivered fatal blows with their broadswords.

Brown made one more stop on his night of terror. He and his men broke into the cabin of James Harris and took hold of a proslavery man named William Sherman, who was living with Harris. They led Sherman to Pottawatomie Creek, slashed his head with their swords, and dumped his dead body into the creek.

Brown's work was finished. In his own mind, he had not committed murder on Pottawatomie Creek that night; he had exacted a just punishment on men who had desired to promote the grievous sin of slavery. Brown believed that by killing these men he had been doing God's great work on earth, by punishing evil men for their sins.

A New Plan

After the killings of the Doyles, Wilkinson, and Sherman, the military authorities responsible for attempting to maintain order

THE CRUSADE AGAINST AMERICAN SLAVERY

Although the abolitionist movement is generally associated with the mid–nineteenth century, individual abolitionist voices were heard in the American colonies as early as the start of the eighteenth century. In 1700 Samuel Sewall, an important businessman and political leader in the Massachusetts Bay Colony, published a pamphlet titled *The Selling of Joseph*, which compared American slavery to the selling of the biblical Joseph into slavery in Egypt by his jealous brothers and which identified the African slaves as "sons of Adam" who "have equal right unto liberty, and all other outward comforts of life." In 1739 a group of antislavery citizens from Darien, Georgia, published an appeal to make slavery illegal in Georgia. In 1789 Benjamin Franklin addressed the Pennsylvania Society for Promoting the Abolition of Slavery with an eloquent oration that identified slavery as "such an atrocious debasement of human nature, that its very extirpation, if not performed with solicitous care, may sometimes open a source of serious evils."

Benjamin Franklin protested slavery in 1789, calling it "an atrocious debasement of human nature."

The abolitionist movement gained momentum after 1820, as a wave of social reform—religious reform, prison reform, educational reform, a women's rights movement—swept the United States. The abolitionist movement included such notables as the writer and editor William Lloyd Garrison, the attorney and orator Wendell Phillips, the minister Lyman Beecher, ex-slaves Frederick Douglass and Sojourner Truth, the author Lydia Child, and the poet John Greenleaf Whittier.

in Kansas issued a warrant for Brown's arrest. But he remained in Kansas to continue the fight against the proslavery forces. And the fury of the battle over Kansas intensified. The territory became known as Bleeding Kansas as a civil war broke out that claimed more than two hundred lives.

One of those killed in combat was Brown's son Frederick. He was gunned down while he returned from an errand at a friend's cabin. Frederick was the first of Brown's sons to die in the war over slavery, but he would not be the last.

Brown remained in Kansas for five months after the killings along Pottawatomie Creek. In the autumn of 1856, a new governor, supported by almost three thousand federal troops, brought some order to Bleeding Kansas. Brown, afraid that he might be arrested for murder, quietly left the territory and headed east. He had begun to form a new plan to strike out against slavery and its defenders. He needed to contact his abolitionist friends in the Midwest and East to recruit men and raise money to put his plan into action.

By this time, Brown was well known in influential abolitionist circles. The news of the killings in Kansas had spread, and every important abolitionist leader wanted to meet the great Captain John Brown. Brown needed their support. He was forming in his mind a plan for a bold stroke that would rid America of slavery forever.

Chapter 2

The Crime

AFTER LEAVING KANSAS in the fall of 1856, John Brown traveled extensively throughout the East and Midwest soliciting funds for a bold new plan to strike a deadly blow against American slavery. He revealed the details of his plan to no one, but to every abolitionist leader he met he made an appeal for funds and recruits. He traveled to Boston and Concord, Massachusetts, where he met William Lloyd Garrison; Theodore Parker, the famous abolitionist minister; and Henry David Thoreau, a writer and orator who had written and spoken eloquently for the abolitionist cause. They, in turn, introduced Brown to other noteworthy abolitionist activists. Brown traveled to New York, where he met Hugh Forbes, an Englishman who had fought in the 1848 revolution in Italy led by Giuseppe Garibaldi; Forbes was anxious to participate in a slave revolution in the United States. Brown was

Writer Henry David Thoreau (pictured) introduced John Brown to other important abolitionists.

30

building a network of supporters whom he could call on when he was ready to put his bold plan into action.

Brown did visit his wife and family at their farm in North Elba, New York, but he had ceased being a full-time farmer and family man. He was now a full-time abolitionist crusader. He began telling his most intimate supporters that he was an instrument in God's hands, selected by God to liberate the slaves and exact on slaveholders God's punishment for their awful sin.

The Conspiracy Begins

Eventually Brown began to reveal some of the broad outline of his plan to his most trusted supporters. It would involve a slave rebellion and would take place somewhere in Virginia. He would need men, weapons, and money. The plan was so ambitious that Brown would need at least two years of work to put it into action.

Early in 1857, however, an event took place that added urgency to Brown's plan. In March the U.S. Supreme Court handed down a decision involving a Missouri slave named Dred Scott. Scott had been taken by his master to live for a time in Illinois and Minnesota. Because Illinois was a free state that outlawed slavery and Minnesota was a territory above the 36°30' latitude mark, Scott filed a lawsuit demanding his freedom; the abolitionist lawyers who took his case argued that he had become a freeman when his master took him to a free state and territory to live. The Court ruled against Scott, asserting that a slave was not a citizen and therefore had no constitutional rights; he could not even legally bring a lawsuit to the Supreme Court. Further, the Court ruled that Congress could not pass a law to prohibit slavery in Minnesota or any other territory, because such a law would violate the Fifth Amendment of the Constitution, which prohibited laws designed to deprive citizens of their property. At the time, slaves were considered their owners' property.

Abolitionists were furious at the Court's decision. If Congress could not outlaw slavery in a U.S. territory, then slavery could continue to spread across the American continent. And if a slave owner could bring one slave to a free state to live, what would prevent that owner from bringing a dozen slaves to a free

In 1857 the Supreme Court ruled that a slave named Dred Scott was not a citizen and therefore not entitled to constitutional rights.

state and holding them in bondage? Could slavery even be introduced in Northern states, where it was legally banned? Abolitionists across the country began to believe that the Slave Power—the influential Southern slaveholding plantation owners and the politicians who represented them—were beginning to dominate American politics. Brown concluded that it was time to deliver a terrible blow against the defenders of slavery.

Recruiting an Army

In the fall of 1857, Brown returned to Lawrence, Kansas. The warfare that had consumed Kansas the previous year had almost ended, so there was no need for Brown to repeat the violent ordeal of the previous year. But Brown had fought with men in Kansas whom he could recruit for his new plan, dedicated abolitionists who did not fear killing or dying for the cause. In Kansas, Brown succeeded in recruiting four men—John Cook, John Henry Kagi, Aaron Stevens, and Charles Moffett. All were devoted abolitionists and veterans of the Kansas wars. Brown arranged to meet the men again in a few weeks in Tabor, Iowa, where he knew some other potential recruits. In Iowa, Brown found several more volunteers, future soldiers in his slave revolution.

By the spring of 1858, Brown was back in the East. In March he assembled a group of dedicated and influential New England and New York abolitionists to whom he began to spell out the details of his great plan. The group, which Brown named the Secret Six, included Gerrit Smith, a wealthy landowner and social reformer from New York; Theodore Parker, the Massachusetts-based Unitarian minister; Thomas Wentworth Higginson, a Massachusetts writer and editor; Franklin Sanborn, a schoolteacher from Concord; Samuel Howe, a Massachusetts physician; and George Luther Stearns, chairman of the Massachusetts Kansas Committee, which had given Brown money for his Kansas crusade. These men had been working more than a decade to eliminate slavery in the United States, only to realize that the Slave Power was gaining strength. Like Brown, they had come to believe that slavery could not be destroyed without the shedding of Southern blood. After forming the Secret Six, Brown wrote ecstatically to a friend that "the slave will be delivered by the shedding of blood, and the signs are multiplying that his deliverance is at hand."

In May, Brown traveled to Chatham, Canada, a town of six thousand residents that included some two thousand escaped African American slaves. Brown gathered a group of the town's black citizens in a Masonic lodge in hope of recruiting some of them in a daring mission that he now announced would take place somewhere in the mountains of western Virginia. It would be a slave rebellion, and Brown appealed to his listeners by providing them with an overview of similar rebellions that had taken place throughout history, including the story of Spartacus, the ancient Roman gladiator who had led a slave revolt against Rome. Brown also released to his audience the articles of his Provisional Constitution and Ordinances for the People of the United States, a legal document that he intended to enact when he began his slave rebellion. The black citizens of Chatham who had gathered to hear Brown were impressed with his vigor and his commitment to the abolitionist cause, but most of them had recently escaped Southern slavery for freedom in Canada and were not anxious to return to the South and risk their lives and liberty in a slave rebellion. A few Canadians, however, did later join Brown's army.

By this time, Brown's closest confidants knew the details of his plan. Brown intended to capture the federal arms arsenal in the small town of Harpers Ferry in western Virginia, near the

JOHN BROWN'S CONSTITUTION

At Harpers Ferry, John Brown intended to commence a massive slave rebellion that would eventually encompass the entire South. He prepared for the day when he would govern a large army of ex-slaves by composing his Provisional Constitution and Ordinances for the People of the United States. The preamble of that document reads as follows:

Whereas, Slavery, throughout its entire existence in the United States, is none other than a most barbarous, unprovoked, and unjustifiable War of one portion of its citizens upon another portion; the only conditions of which are perpetual imprisonment, and hopeless servitude or absolute extermination; in utter disregard and violation of those eternal and self-evident truths set forth in our Declaration of Independence: Therefore,

We, Citizens of the United States, and the Oppressed People, who, by a recent decision of the Supreme Court are declared to have no rights which the White Man is bound to respect; together with all other people degraded by the laws thereof, Do, for the time being ordain and establish for ourselves, the following PROVISIONAL CONSTITUTION and ORDINANCES, the better to protect our Persons, Property, Lives, and Liberties; and to govern our actions.

Maryland border. He would first liberate the slaves on nearby plantations and arm them with the weapons that he captured. His slave army would spread through Maryland and Virginia, freeing and arming other slaves as they went. From Virginia, the uprising would spread southward until the entire South was in a state of rebellion.

As more people learned the general outline and particular details of Brown's plan, a serious problem developed that would delay its enactment. Hugh Forbes, the Englishman with whom Brown had shared much of his plan, began to have serious doubts about Brown's enterprise. Forbes was still dedicated to the abolitionist cause, but he did not believe that Brown and a small band of followers could ignite a slave rebellion that would end slavery in the United States. Forbes began to leak some of the details of Brown's plan to influential antislavery politicians in Washington.

Fearful that Brown's plan would reach the secretary of war, members of the Secret Six urged Brown to postpone his mission and return to Kansas to create some diversion that would convince the politicians who had spoken with Forbes that Brown's Harpers Ferry plan was little more than a fantastic rumor. So in the spring of 1858, Brown again headed for Lawrence, Kansas, to mislead anyone who was plotting against him.

A Practice Run in Kansas

When Brown arrived in Kansas in June 1858, the territory was relatively peaceful. The slavery question in Kansas was to be settled at the ballot box rather than on the battlefield. In August, Kansans would go to the polls and vote for or against the Lecompton Constitution, which would allow slavery in the territory. When the election came, Kansas voters overwhelmingly defeated the proslavery constitution. When Kansas came into the Union, which would not happen for another three years, it would be admitted as a free state.

But Brown still saw work to be done in Kansas besides creating a diversion for the Harpers Ferry plan. He continued in earnest to recruit volunteers to join him the following year at Harpers Ferry. He managed to attract two veterans of the Kansas wars, Jeremiah Anderson and Albert Hazlett.

One day in December, while in Kansas, Brown was presented with an opportunity to engage in the kind of activity that he was planning for Harpers Ferry. George Gill, one of Brown's Kansas recruits, met a runaway slave from across the Kansas border in Missouri. The man claimed that he had run off because his family was about to be broken up and sold. Gill brought the man to Brown, who obtained directions to the slave's owner's farm. On the night of December 20, Brown led a band of his men across the border into Missouri. Brown and his men invaded two farms, liberating eleven slaves, killing one owner, capturing two others, and confiscating horses and wagons. They led the freed slaves into Kansas and hid them in the town of Osawatomie. Eventually, Brown and his men helped the ex-slaves reach freedom in Canada.

The word quickly spread that old John Brown—now known as Osawatomie Brown—was again creating havoc in Kansas. The proslavery press accused Brown of trying to start another war in Kansas. President James Buchanan demanded Brown's arrest and put a bounty price of $250 on his head. (Brown later retaliated by placing a price of $2.50 on the head of President Buchanan.) Brown's followers and supporters were excited. They reasoned that if Brown could free slaves in Missouri, he could free slaves in Virginia as well.

The time had come for Brown to execute his Harpers Ferry plan. He had already sent one of his lieutenants, John Cook, to Harpers Ferry to get a job there and to scout the town and surrounding region. In early January of 1859, Brown and his company left Kansas and headed eastward.

Settling in Harpers Ferry

Brown returned to Boston to meet the members of his Secret Six and ask for money, arms, and recruits. He attended a convention of the New England Anti-Slavery Society, but he was disappointed with the event. "Talk! talk! talk!" he complained. "That will never free the slaves. What is needed is action— action." After the conference, he visited a prominent abolitionist judge named Thomas Russell. During the visit, Brown lifted Russell's young daughter so that she stood in the palm of his hand. "Now when you are a young lady and I am hanged, you can say that you stood on the hand of Old Brown," he told the child.

From Boston, Brown traveled south to Collinsville, Connecticut, where he had earlier contracted with a man to construct five hundred pikes—inexpensive spears with which he could arm the slaves after the rebellion began. Then he made one more visit to his wife and children in North Elba, New York, and departed for Harpers Ferry.

Harpers Ferry was a small town in the Blue Ridge Mountains of western Virginia set on a narrow tract of land at the intersection of two powerful rivers, the Shenandoah and Potomac. The water from the two rivers powered the mills in the factories

A HISTORY OF HARPERS FERRY

In 1794 Congress passed the Armory Act of 1794, establishing a federal armory in Harpers Ferry, where military weaponry could be manufactured and housed. The small Virginia town was chosen as the site by President George Washington for three reasons. First, Harpers Ferry was only seventy-five miles from the new capital in Washington, D.C. Second, the town was built at the intersection of two powerful rivers, the Potomac and Shenandoah, which could power the machinery needed in the weapons factories. Third, Harpers Ferry, wedged between the two rivers and high cliffs known as Bolivar Heights, would be easy to defend if the United States was ever invaded.

The Harpers Ferry armory was producing its first weapons by 1801. Eventually the munitions plant comprised more than twenty buildings and produced more than ten thousand weapons per year. Meriwether Lewis and William Clark carried weapons manufactured at Harpers Ferry on their great 1804–1806 exploration of the lands acquired in the Louisiana Purchase.

During the 1830s the Baltimore & Ohio Railroad laid tracks through Harpers Ferry, connecting it to Baltimore and Washington to the east and Ohio to the west, ensuring the town's survival as a thriving commercial center. In 1861, however, the Civil War came, bringing havoc and destruction upon Harpers Ferry. At the start of the war, most of the armory buildings were burned by federal troops to prevent them from falling into the hands of the Confederates. The town exchanged hands several times during the course of the war, and extensive damage occurred during each takeover.

After the war, the weapons factories were never rebuilt, so few economic opportunities existed in Harpers Ferry. A series of devastating floods occurred during the final decades of the nineteenth century, dissuading investors from rebuilding the town into the industrial center that it had been before the war.

Today much of Harpers Ferry, now in the state of West Virginia, has been set aside as a national park. Each year it attracts thousands of visitors, who come to see the site of John Brown's rebellion and to learn about small-town American life during the nineteenth century.

in which guns and other weapons were made for the federal army. The Baltimore & Ohio Railroad passed through the town and ran westward through the Allegheny Mountains and into Ohio. In 1859 Harpers Ferry's population was about twenty-five hundred, half of whom were free black residents. Fewer than

This view of Harpers Ferry shows the confluence of the Shenandoah and Potomac Rivers. John Brown arrived here in hopes of leading a slave rebellion to capture a U.S. military arsenal.

one hundred slaves worked on nearby farms, though thousands of slaves labored in the surrounding counties.

Brown arrived at Harpers Ferry in early July and rented a farmhouse owned by a Dr. Booth Kennedy on the Maryland side of the Potomac River. Some of his recruits had already arrived, and several more would move in during the coming months. Brown's army would eventually comprise twenty-two men, including himself. Brown was somewhat disappointed that more volunteers were not coming. Men whom he had met earlier and to whom he had written failed to respond to his urgent call to come to Harpers Ferry. Brown was particularly disappointed that Frederick Douglass, the great African American writer and orator, had decided not to join the forthcoming slave rebellion.

Some Doubters

Actually, some of Brown's supporters, including Douglass, had begun to have doubts about his plan. They were skeptical of Brown's ability to capture and hold a federal weapons arsenal, and they were doubtful whether hundreds of thousands of slaves were ready to join a slave rebellion. In August 1859, three of Brown's friends from Iowa, fearful that Brown was embarking on a mission that would end in disaster, sent an anonymous letter to Secretary of War John Floyd informing him of most of the details of the Harpers Ferry plan. Floyd, however, believed the letter to be a hoax; he could not imagine that any sane man would attempt such a risky mission.

Brown, however, had great confidence in his plan; he reasoned that the Harpers Ferry arsenal was guarded by only a handful of men, and the nearest company of federal troops was stationed in Washington, D.C., seventy-five miles away. Moreover, having met Frederick Douglass and other ex-slaves who had escaped from their masters, Brown was convinced that thousands of slaves were seething in anger and resentment over their condition and were waiting for the proper moment to turn on their owners and set themselves free. Brown figured that with a little assistance these slaves would readily rise up, slay their masters, and fight to assist other slaves in gaining their freedom. Brown did consider the possibility that he might fail, but he told his recruits, "We have here

The schoolhouse where John Brown stored his weapons in anticipation of his slave rebellion.

only one life to live, and once to die; and if we lose our lives it will
perhaps do more for the cause than our lives would be worth the
other way." Brown expected that other abolitionists would follow
his lead, even if he failed at Harpers Ferry.

Brown stayed the course. He told his Harpers Ferry neighbors that he was intending to raise cattle, and he kept his recruits
hidden in the attic of his farmhouse. As the months passed and
Brown waited for the perfect moment to make his attack, he laid
out a careful plan and assigned each man a role in the mission.
Brown quizzed his men frequently about their tasks; he wanted
no errors at the time of the mission. As he waited, supplies of
weapons that Brown had ordered during the previous months
began to reach Harpers Ferry. He hid them well; he expected
that they would soon be put to good use.

The Raid Commences

The final three recruits in Brown's army reached his Maryland
farmhouse on October 15. One recruit, Francis Jackson Meriam,
had $600 in gold to contribute to Brown's cause. Brown saw this
good fortune as a sign from God that the time for action had
arrived. On the next evening, a Sunday evening, Brown gathered his troops, loaded a wagon with weapons, and rode out
toward Harpers Ferry. He left three men at the Kennedy farmhouse as a rear guard.

The night was chilly and overcast, with an occasional drizzle
in the air. But the weather would not hamper Brown. He and his
men moved with determined precision toward Harpers Ferry.
When they got close to town, Brown ordered the telegraph lines
to be cut so that no message of alarm could be sent out when
Brown began his work.

By about nine o'clock, Brown's men were approaching the
covered wooden bridge that crossed the Potomac River at
Harpers Ferry. Brown sent two men ahead to apprehend the
night watchman. Having gained control of one entrance to the
town, Brown sent two more men to capture the Shenandoah
River bridge. He now controlled both gateways into Harpers
Ferry; the town would soon be his.

John Brown and his volunteers begin their raid on Harpers Ferry.

Quickly and quietly, Brown's soldiers moved through town and approached the armory and arsenal buildings, where thousands of weapons were held for the federal army. The arms buildings were guarded by a single sentry, whom Brown's men surprised and apprehended. "I came here from Kansas, and this is a slave state," Brown reportedly told the frightened security guard. "I want to free all the negroes in this state; I have possession now of the United States armory, and if the citizens interfere with me I must only burn the town and have blood." Brown moved his wagon into the armory compound and left several men to guard the facility.

Brown's next target was Hall's Rifle Works, a rifle factory located on Shenandoah Street on the other end of town, about a half mile from the armory buildings. Brown captured the factory, left two men to guard it, then returned to the armory buildings on Potomac Street, where he would set up his command post. So far, everything was working out just as Brown had planned. In less than two hours, Brown had gained control of both bridges leading into and out of Harpers Ferry, and he had seized control of buildings housing thousands of weapons.

At this time, the rear guard left behind at the Kennedy farmhouse loaded leftover weapons into a wagon and embarked for a nearby schoolhouse. They would spread the word to the slaves on local farms to flee and rendezvous at the schoolhouse to pick up a weapon and obtain orders for further action.

Back at Harpers Ferry, Brown deployed six men on a mission five miles outside Harpers Ferry. An hour before midnight, the six invaders embarked for the farm of Colonel Lewis Washington, a great-grandnephew of George Washington. Brown wanted this influential Harpers Ferry citizen to be taken hostage and his slaves freed. Brown's soldiers burst into Washington's home around midnight and easily captured him. They searched his house for weapons and found a fine military sword, a gift to George Washington from Frederick the Great, king of Prussia. Colonel Washington and his ten slaves were put into a wagon and taken to Harpers Ferry. Washington would be held as a captive; his slaves would be armed to take part in the rebellion. Other influential Harpers Ferry citizens were awakened and taken into custody by Brown's men.

The First Problem

Sometime after midnight, the first problem developed. Patrick Higgins, another night watchman, was scheduled to relieve the watchman taken prisoner earlier at the Potomac River bridge. Not knowing what had occurred earlier in the evening, Higgins approached the bridge expecting to relieve his co-worker and fulfill his nightly guard duties. As he approached the bridge, one of Brown's men fired a shot at him, though Brown had specifically ordered that shots should not be fired except in self-defense. The bullet pierced his hat, grazed his scalp, and sent him scurrying away from the bridge. Higgins ran for safety to Wager House, a Harpers Ferry hotel and railroad station. The frightened Higgins told his story to anyone awake who would listen. The shot through the still night had woken some citizens, who began to emerge from their sleeping quarters to see what was happening.

At 1:30 another serious problem developed for Brown when the train en route from Wheeling, Virginia, to Baltimore approached Harpers Ferry. Brown wanted the train to pass through town unimpeded, but when it stopped at Wager House to pick up a passenger, Higgins warned the conductor that armed men were guarding the Potomac River bridge, which the train had to cross to exit Harpers Ferry. The conductor, fearing a robbery, decided not to press on.

A Death at Harpers Ferry

After the train stopped, the conductor and several other men at Wager House decided to walk up the tracks and see what was going on ahead at the bridge. John Brown's son Oliver, stationed at the bridge, saw the approaching party and demanded that they halt. He fired a warning shot and the men began to retreat. One man, however, a baggage handler named Hayward Shepherd, moved forward. William Thompson, stationed at the bridge with Oliver Brown, fired at Shepherd, and the bullet found its target. The other men helped Shepherd back to Wager House and attempted to treat him, but the wound was fatal. The first death had occurred at Harpers Ferry. Ironically, Shepherd was black, a freeman popular among the Harpers Ferry townspeople.

Brown was still in control, but his position would soon deteriorate. Many of the local citizens had been awakened by the commotion in their generally peaceful town and were roaming the streets of Harpers Ferry with weapons in hand. A hostage whom Brown had released to speak with the train conductor had informed the men at Wager House of Brown's grand plan, and the citizens of Harpers Ferry were prepared to repel the invaders and take back their town. Near dawn Brown allowed the train to leave Harpers Ferry on the condition that the conductor not say anything of the rebellion, but the conductor spread the word at his subsequent train stops. The telegraph wires were soon spreading word of the events at Harpers Ferry throughout Maryland and Virginia. As the word of Brown's rebellion spread, his actions were greatly exaggerated. Some reported that he had already armed hundreds of slaves, who were roaming the countryside. Citizens who had remembered Nat Turner's rebellion twenty-eight years earlier were preparing themselves for the coming slave revolt. News of the Harpers Ferry insurrection soon reached President James Buchanan in Washington.

By Monday morning, the Jefferson Guards of the Virginia militia had been alerted to the uprising at Harpers Ferry. The Guards, stationed several miles away in Charles Town, marched to Harpers Ferry to rescue the town and its citizens. By eleven o'clock they were near the town. The militiamen soon routed Brown's bridge guards and poured into Harpers Ferry. The soldiers and armed civilians began firing on Brown's headquarters at the armory buildings. Brown, surprised by how quickly an opposing force had mobilized, moved his hostages—there were more than a dozen by now—into a fire-engine house in the armory yard.

During this melee, one of Brown's recruits, Dangerfield Newby—a free black man hoping to free his wife and children, who were held in bondage on a Virginia plantation—was struck in the neck by a bullet. The shot sliced Newby's throat, and he quickly died on the street. Seeing Newby lying dead, one

The arsenal at Harpers Ferry, where Brown and his volunteers would take their stand against the Virginia militia.

Harpers Ferry resident approached the body with a large knife and cut off Newby's ears to save as souvenirs of the great event that was unfolding.

Trapped in Harpers Ferry

Brown soon sensed that he was trapped. Harpers Ferry was an easy town to defend because of its location, but it was also an easy place in which to get trapped. Brown's enemies had control of the two bridges that led out of town. To Brown's back were two wide rivers, and he had no boats available on which to escape via the water. Directly outside the town were Bolivar Heights, large cliffs that would be difficult to scale if Brown chose to fight his way across town.

Brown decided to propose a deal. He would release all hostages unharmed if he and his men were allowed safe passage out of town. He sent Will Thompson out of the fire-engine house under a flag of truce to negotiate with the men surrounding him, but Thompson was apprehended and held captive at Wager House. Brown then sent out two more negotiators, his son Watson and Aaron Stevens, but the two men were shot. Stevens was taken prisoner, and Watson crawled back to the engine house seriously wounded.

During lulls in the action, many of the militiamen and citizens had been visiting Galt House, a saloon near the hotel. They were calling for blood, demanding that Brown and his followers be quickly apprehended and executed on the spot. One of Brown's men, William Leeman, sensing their impossible situation, decided to make a run for it toward the Potomac River. He jumped into the water and made his way to a small island, where an angry mob of Harpers Ferry residents apprehended him and instantly shot him dead. For a time, Leeman's body remained where he had fallen, and drunken militiamen used the corpse for target practice.

Soon afterward, a crowd of armed citizens surrounded Hall's Rifle Works, where three of Brown's men were stationed. The men decided to abandon the factory and make a run for it. John Henry Kagi was shot dead as he rushed toward the Shenandoah

River; Lewis Leary was shot and captured; and John Copeland was also apprehended.

Though reduced in number, Brown's men fought back. They killed a slave owner named George Turner. They wounded several militiamen. Then, later in the afternoon, one of Brown's men fired upon a citizen who was walking along the railroad tracks. Mayor Fontaine Beckham of Harpers Ferry immediately fell dead. Beckham's death enabled Brown to partly achieve his goal. In his will, the mayor had decreed that five of his slaves would be set free upon his death. They would be the only slaves freed during Brown's rebellion.

Two of Brown's men escaped and rushed to the schoolhouse to warn the three raiders Brown had stationed there to guard the weapons and arm escaped slaves. The rear guard and the two men who had fled Harpers Ferry made a run for it.

But Brown was trapped. Two more of his troops were wounded. By Monday evening he and seven of his men were surrounded in the fire-engine house along with a dozen hostages. Brown's sons Watson and Oliver were fatally wounded and suffering intense pain. Oliver would die before the night was over and Watson two days later. More militia companies from the surrounding towns had answered the alarm and had arrived at Harpers Ferry ready to fight. Brown was in no position to negotiate; he would either have to surrender or wait for the inevitable assault on the fire-engine house.

Colonel Lee Arrives

Early Monday morning, when President Buchanan had heard the news of the attack on Harpers Ferry, he had dispatched to the town a battalion of ninety U.S. Marines under the command of Colonel Robert E. Lee, an able West Point graduate who had been tested on the battlefield during the Mexican War. By early Tuesday morning, Lee's troops had reached Harpers Ferry. Colonel Lee immediately assumed control of all military personnel in the town. During the evening, Brown's men who were pinned inside the engine house had removed a few bricks to use as gun holes. At dawn when the men peered through the holes,

ROBERT E. LEE: VIRGINIA'S NATIVE SON

The military commander summoned to put down John Brown's uprising at Harpers Ferry was a Virginia native, born in 1807, into a famous military family. Lee's father, Henry "Light-Horse Harry" Lee had served heroically as a cavalry commander under General George Washington during the American Revolution. In 1829 the younger Lee graduated from the United States Military Academy at West Point and, following his father's lead, began an impressive military career.

Lee first engaged in combat during the Mexican War, while he served under General Winfield Scott during the campaign against Mexico City. Lee distinguished himself during crucial battles at Cerro Gordo and Chapultepec and earned a promotion to the rank of colonel. After the Mexican War, Lee served for three years as superintendent at West Point. Lee was living at his family estate in Arlington, Virginia, when he was ordered by President James Buchanan to quell the uprising at Harpers Ferry.

For Lee, however, the engagement at Harpers Ferry would prove to be a minor skirmish when compared with the battles that he would fight in the future. In 1861 Lee declined an offer by General Scott to lead the federal forces in subduing another rebellion, this one begun by several Southern states that had seceded from the Union. When his home state of Virginia seceded and joined the Confederate States of America, Lee declined Scott's offer and accepted an offer by Jefferson Davis, president of the Confederacy, to command the Army of Northern Virginia.

Lee performed brilliantly during the Civil War. Often outnumbered in battle, Lee was rarely outmaneuvered. He executed astonishing victories during the Seven Days' Battles, at the Second Battle of Bull Run, at Fredericksburg, and, most impressively, at Chancellorsville, where he used unorthodox and daring tactics to defeat a Union force almost twice the size of his army.

But in July 1863, after a string of impressive battlefield victories, Lee was stopped by Union forces at Gettysburg and administered a terrible defeat. His army never recovered, and Lee was forced to surrender his troops to General Ulysses S. Grant at Appomattox Court House, Virginia, in April 1865.

After the war, Lee pledged his support to the Union, retired from military life, and served as president of Washington College in Virginia. He died in 1870.

Colonel Lee's capable assistant at Harpers Ferry, J. E. B. Stuart, became one of his most trustworthy generals during the Civil War. Stuart commanded Lee's cavalry until 1864, when he was fatally wounded during an engagement at Yellow Tavern, Virginia.

they saw an impressive deployment of federal troops surrounding the armory compound.

Lee did not immediately attack. He sent his lieutenant, J. E. B. Stuart, who had met Brown while serving in Kansas in 1856, toward the fire-engine house under a flag of truce. Stuart demanded an unconditional surrender at once. Brown tried to bargain, offering to surrender the armory and release his hostages unharmed if he and his men were allowed to leave town unimpeded. Lee responded to Brown's offer by ordering an attack.

Lee's troops stormed the building, ramming down the door with a heavy ladder. Two of Brown's men were bayoneted to death. Lieutenant Israel Green attacked Brown with a sword, slicing the older man and thrusting at Brown's abdomen. Green's sword, however, struck Brown's belt buckle and bent. Green beat Brown across the head with the hilt of his sword, and Brown fell unconscious.

Brown's slave rebellion was over. Ten of Brown's men had been killed or were fatally wounded and would die within two

Federal troops enter the federal arsenal to capture John Brown and his remaining rebels.

Lieutenant Israel Green hits John Brown over the head with the hilt of his sword to subdue him.

days. Brown and four others were taken captive. Seven men, including the rear guard, had escaped, but two of the runaways would be captured fleeing through Pennsylvania during the next week. (The remaining five escapees would never be apprehended.) Four local residents had lost their lives during the uprising, including the mayor of Harpers Ferry, and one of Colonel Lee's troops had been killed. None of the slaves living on the nearby farms had been freed. Those who had been liberated from Colonel Washington's plantation on Sunday night returned to their home, swearing that they had been compelled by Brown's men to escape. On Tuesday afternoon, October 18, 1859, it seemed as though Brown's great campaign to end American slavery had ended in dismal failure.

Chapter 3

The Trial

JOHN BROWN'S ATTEMPT to end American slavery by igniting a slave rebellion in Harpers Ferry, Virginia, had indeed failed. Most of his recruits had been killed or captured, and no slaves had taken up arms against their masters. But even as he lay wounded and defeated on October 18, 1859, Brown sensed an opportunity to turn his tragedy into triumph. Had he been killed at Harpers Ferry, he and his raid might be quickly forgotten. But Brown believed that God had spared him so that he might have another chance to deliver his antislavery message to the American people. A courtroom trial would provide Brown with a forum from which to announce to the country the purpose of his Harpers Ferry endeavor. Then, perhaps, other abolitionist leaders might continue his work.

Brown's trial, from arraignment through sentencing, would last only nine days. Nonetheless, the entire country would pay heed to the courtroom drama that took place in Charles Town, Virginia, from October 25 through November 2, 1859. Brown would use the courtroom, his jail cell, and later the gallows as pulpits from which to sermonize to the American people on the righteousness of his cause.

A Conversation with the Governor

On Tuesday afternoon, Brown, held captive in one of the armory buildings, regained consciousness. He was in great pain, but he was alert and aware of what was going on about him. His guard asked if he was well enough to see visitors, and Brown replied that he was. Into Brown's makeshift jail stepped several men—Virginia governor Henry Wise, Virginia senator James Mason, Representative Clement Vallandigham of Ohio, Colonel Robert E. Lee and Lieutenant J. E. B. Stuart, Lewis Washington, and a handful of reporters. The politicians and reporters had quickstepped to Harpers Ferry when news of Brown's attempted takeover spread to Washington. Governor Wise politely asked Brown if he would mind answering some questions about his business at Harpers Ferry, and the prisoner readily agreed. Brown knew that reporters were present to record his every word.

Governor Wise and Senator Mason tried to get Brown to divulge the names of any of his conspirators; they were anxious to know whether prominent abolitionists were aware of his plans or had provided Brown with money or weapons. To their questions about his sponsors, Brown simply replied, "I will answer freely and faithfully about what concerns *myself*. I will answer anything I can with honor, but not about others."

After some questions about Brown's activities in Kansas years before, Senator Mason asked Brown about his present escapade. "Now, sir, how do you justify your acts?" the senator asked. Brown had a ready response. "I think, my friend," replied Brown, "you are guilty of a great wrong against God and humanity—I say it without wishing to be offensive—and that it would be perfectly right in anyone to interfere with you so as to free those you wickedly and willfully hold in bondage."

The questions strayed to other topics, but a young

Senator James Mason (pictured) was among those who questioned John Brown about the reasons for his actions. Brown remained unrepentant.

reporter in the back of the room, sensing the importance of Brown's commitment to his cause, asked Brown if he saw himself as the leader in some kind of religious movement. "It is, in my opinion, the greatest service a man can render to God," replied Brown. When the reporter asked Brown to provide the religious principle upon which he could justify his actions at Harpers Ferry, Brown responded, "Upon the Golden Rule. That is why I am here. Not to gratify any personal animosity, revenge, or vindictiveness. It is my sympathy with the oppressed and the wronged—that are as good as you—and as precious in the sight of God." Brown, speaking with the force of a preacher, elaborated further on this idea.

> I want you to understand, gentlemen, and I want you to report that I respect the rights of the poorest and weakest colored people, oppressed by the slave system, just as much as I do those of the most wealthy and powerful. This is the idea that has moved me, and that alone. We expect no reward, except the satisfaction of doing for those in distress and greatly oppressed, as we would be done by. The cry of distress of the oppressed is my reason, and the only thing that prompted me to come here.

As the interview continued, Brown began to lose strength, and the governor and his party saw that it was time to leave the room. One reporter asked Brown if he had anything else to add. He assured Brown that he would print whatever message Brown wished to deliver. Again the weary prisoner saw the opportunity to lecture his listeners—and the readers of the reporter's newspaper—on the evils of slavery:

> I have nothing to say, only that I claim to be here carrying out a measure I believe perfectly justifiable and not to act the part of an incendiary or ruffian, but to aid those suffering great wrong. I wish to say, furthermore, that you had better—all you people at the South—prepare yourselves for a settlement of that question that must come up much sooner than you are prepared for. The sooner you are prepared, the better. You may dispose of

me very easily; I am nearly disposed of now. But this question is still to be settled—this Negro Question, I mean—the end of that is not yet.

The interview concluded a few minutes later.

The Charges

Governor Wise wanted a speedy trial for John Brown. He feared that Brown would either be seized by a lynch mob and executed without a trial or rescued by his abolitionist backers. To better guard Brown, Governor Wise ordered him transferred to a jail several miles away in Charles Town, Virginia, where the Jefferson Guards were headquartered. A county circuit court was already in session in Charles Town, and Governor Wise wanted Brown tried in that court. Brown should properly have been turned over to federal authorities—because he had seized federal property at Harpers Ferry. But Governor Wise wanted the state of Virginia to try Brown. The governor reasoned that a trial in Virginia could be conducted more rapidly than a federal trial. Furthermore, Governor Wise sensed that he could earn some political perks by prosecuting and executing Brown according to Virginia law. Wise appointed Andrew Hunter as the special prosecutor in the case.

Brown's arraignment was set for October 25, only one week after his capture. That would not provide him with very much time to prepare an adequate defense. But the early trial date did not seem to bother Brown. "I am ready for my fate," he told reporters. "I do not ask a trial. I beg for no mockery of a trial, no insult—nothing but that which conscience gives, or cowardice would drive you to practice." Brown was assigned two local defense lawyers, but he viewed them with disinterest. "I do not care anything about counsel," he said. "It is unnecessary to trouble any gentleman with that duty." Nonetheless, on October 21, Brown, from his jail cell, had written to his friend Judge Thomas Russell in Massachusetts and to some friends in Ohio "to obtain able and faithful counsel for myself and fellow prisoners." He explained that he did not want to be defended by Southern lawyers.

ESCAPE PLOTS

During the six weeks between John Brown's arrest and execution, his abolitionist friends and supporters from around the United States discussed the idea of rescuing him with some daredevil escape plan. George Hoyt, the young lawyer from Massachusetts dispatched to Virginia to defend Brown, was charged by Brown's backers to assess the possibility of arranging an escape. Hoyt sent to his Massachusetts associates a sketch of the prison compound in Charles Town where Brown was being held captive. The sketch—which identified the buildings where Brown and his recruits were imprisoned, the location of the jailer, and the height of the wall surrounding the prison compound—was later published in the *New York Tribune*, an antislavery newspaper. By publishing the sketch, the newspaper's editors hoped to encourage some daring abolitionists to attempt to rescue Brown and his men from jail.

Brown's friend Judge Thomas Russell of Massachusetts came to visit Brown in his Charles Town jail cell after the trial. Russell made the trip to Virginia mainly to comfort Brown during the final weeks of his life. But Russell was also scouting the territory to see if an escape plan was feasible. Russell concluded that Brown was well guarded and that it would take a bold and imaginative plan to spring the prisoner free.

Some of the escape plans discussed by abolitionist factions were indeed fantastic. One called for the kidnapping of Governor Henry Wise, who would then be exchanged for Brown. Another escape plot called for armed men on horseback to intercept Brown as he was led to the gallows on December 2. Thomas Higginson, one of the Secret Six who had helped finance Brown's Harpers Ferry invasion, traveled to Brown's farm in North Elba, New York, and convinced Brown's wife, Mary, to travel to Charles Town to inform her husband that plans were being laid for his rescue and to convince him to cooperate with his rescuers.

Actually, Brown did not wish to be rescued. If he escaped, he would be forced to flee the country or live a secret life of disguise, and he would not be able to speak out publicly against slavery. If he was to hang, however, Brown would be able to use his jail cell and the gallows as forums from which to continue to rail against slavery's evils. Hence, Brown preferred the gallows to rescue, and his wishes were granted.

At about two o'clock in the afternoon on October 25, Brown and four of his Harpers Ferry raiders, still dressed in the same rumpled clothes that they wore during the raid, were brought into the red-brick colonial-style courthouse in Charles Town for arraignment, with Judge Richard Parker presiding. Militiamen guarded the jail where Brown was held as well as the courthouse. A contingent escorted the prisoners into the courtroom. The trial had attracted a great many visitors to Charles Town, many of whom gathered outside the courthouse shouting for immediate justice. The militia prepared to defend Brown and his followers against a lynch mob, but the arraignment proceeded quickly and smoothly.

Judge Parker provided instructions to the grand jury, which returned the next day charging Brown and his men with murdering five people, conspiring to ignite a slave rebellion, and committing treason against Virginia. Brown and his four surviving raiders all pleaded not guilty to the charges. Then Brown requested that he be tried separately from the others; he wished to stand alone as a defendant so that the public's attention would be focused solely on himself. The court agreed to that request but denied his next one: for a delay until he had fully recovered from the wounds that he had received when Colonel Lee's troops invaded the fire-engine house. A trial jury was quickly selected, and the trial was scheduled to begin the next day, October 27.

John Brown and his fellow rebels are arraigned in court. They all pleaded not guilty to the charges brought against them.

The Trial Begins

On October 27 Brown was brought into the crowded courtroom on a cot. He claimed that he was too weak to walk into the courtroom and sit upright during his trial. Immediately after the trial began, Lawson Botts, one of Brown's court-appointed defense attorneys, surprised everyone in the courtroom, including Brown, by approaching the judge's bench and requesting that the trial be suspended. Botts claimed that Brown was insane. He read a telegram, from an Ohio friend of the Brown family, that asserted that Brown's mother's sister died of insanity and that her daughter had been committed to an insane asylum. Hence, Botts maintained that Brown, too, was affected by this family malady.

Brown vigorously rejected Botts's insanity plea. "I will add, if the Court will allow me, that I look upon it as a miserable artifice and pretext of those who ought to take a different course in regard to me," stated Brown. "I view it with contempt more than otherwise." Brown argued that insane people have little ability to judge their own sanity. "I am perfectly unconscious of insanity,"

During the trial, spectators crowd the gallery as John Brown, too weak to stand, lies on a cot in the center of the courtroom. Brown vigorously rejected his lawyer's attempts to introduce the insanity defense.

he continued, "and I reject, so far as I am capable, any attempt to interfere in my behalf on that score." Brown did not want those watching the trial to think that attempting to free the slaves was the action of a man who was mentally unbalanced; he believed it perfectly sane to assist slaves in gaining their freedom.

Judge Parker denied Botts's request, and he allowed the prosecution to bring forward its case against Brown. But first, Parker ordered the jury to be fair and "not allow their hatred of abolitionists to influence them against those who have raised the black flag on the soil of this Commonwealth."

Andrew Hunter called to the witness stand a host of Harpers Ferry citizens to testify against Brown. One of the first men called to testify was the conductor of the train that had passed through Harpers Ferry on the night of the raid. The conductor revealed to the court that Brown had described to him the provisional government that Brown had intended to set up after the slave rebellion gained momentum. Indeed, Brown's Provisional Constitution and Ordinances and other documents concerning the raid on Harpers Ferry had been seized by the local sheriff when he had searched the Kennedy farmhouse after Brown's capture. The train conductor, recounting the conversation that he had had with Brown on the night of the raid, informed the court that Brown's provisional government was supposed to include a secretary of state, secretary of war, Supreme Court, and House of Representatives. Murmurs erupted in the crowded courtroom when the details of Brown's plans became known. The courtroom spectators and members of the jury reasoned that Brown was clearly trying to overthrow the U.S. government and set up his own. This was high treason—a crime punishable by execution.

Lewis Washington was then called to the witness stand. He recounted to the court how he had been kidnapped in the middle of the night from his home and, along with his slaves, taken prisoner by Brown's men. He corroborated the train conductor's testimony by explaining to the court the plans of Brown's provisional government, information that Brown had revealed to Washington while Washington was held hostage. Several more witnesses were called, all detailing the events of the previous week at Harpers Ferry. Brown and his lawyers did not dispute any of the testimony rendered. During the entire proceeding, Brown lay on his cot, resting but remaining alert to what was happening in the courtroom.

The Second Day

After the court recessed for the day, a young lawyer, George Hoyt, arrived by train to Charles Town from Massachusetts. Hoyt had been sent by Brown's Massachusetts backers, and his charges went beyond defending Brown in court. If given the opportunity, Hoyt was supposed to seize the letters and other documents that might implicate Brown's supporters in the conspiracy. Brown's backers did not know that the incriminating materials had already been seized by the local authorities. Hoyt was also asked to determine whether any rescue attempt was possible.

On the second day of the trial, the prosecution put forward more witnesses to testify against Brown. Brown was feeling stronger that day, and he cross-examined some of the witnesses

Defense lawyer George Hoyt questions John Brown during his trial. Hoyt had been hired not only to defend Brown, but also to seize any incriminating evidence and determine if his client could be rescued.

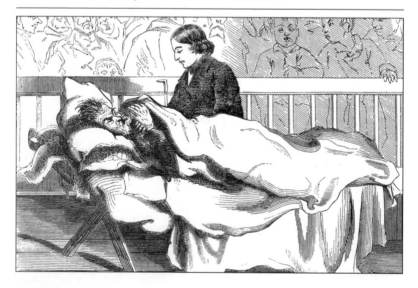

himself. Under Brown's questioning, most of the hostages stated that they had been treated kindly and not harmed in any way. A few witnesses explained to the court that Brown seemed sincere when he told them that he wished to free the Harpers Ferry slaves but not harm any of its citizens.

Also on the trial's second day, the prosecution entered as evidence a carpetbag filled with documents—Brown's Provisional Constitution and Ordinances, military manuals that Brown had composed for his future slave army, and letters from his backers. Many of the documents were read aloud in court as they were entered as evidence. After the sheriff read each document, Brown shouted out "That is mine" so that the entire courtroom could hear him.

During the afternoon of the second day, the prosecution rested its case. Now it would be Brown's turn to defend himself and his actions—before the members of the jury and the American people.

Brown's Defense

Defending Brown would be a formidable task for any attorney. Brown could not deny or even question the testimony of the prosecution's witnesses. Brown had, indeed, taken custody of the federal armory at Harpers Ferry. He had kidnapped people and held them hostage against their will. He and his men had caused the deaths of five people and had wounded several others. And he had certainly conspired to begin a slave rebellion that would spread throughout the South. Brown would have to attempt to persuade the court that he had actually acted righteously and humanely when he committed the crimes with which he was charged.

Brown's first witness was Joseph Brua, one of the Harpers Ferry men held hostage. Brown was acting as his own attorney now. He felt even stronger than he had on the previous day. He moved around the courtroom, focusing his penetrating steel blue eyes on each witness and on the members of the jury. With tough questions he got Brua to testify that Brown had tried to negotiate peacefully before any killing took place and that Brown's negotiators had been shot down while carrying a flag of truce.

*As he grew stronger, John Brown acted
as his own attorney.*

Brown, anxious to drive home
to the jury the idea that the
residents of Harpers Ferry
had acted more cruelly than
he and his men, called Henry
Hunter to the witness stand,
the prosecuting attorney's
son. The younger Hunter had
killed William Thompson,
one of Brown's men, by
shooting him at point-blank
range on the Potomac River
bridge and then throwing his
body into the water. Hunter
detailed his grisly work to the
court and concluded his testimony by explaining that his
uncle, Mayor Beckham of
Harpers Ferry, and one of his
best friends had already been shot down "by those villainous abolitionists" and that he therefore "felt justified in shooting any that I
could find. I felt it was my duty and have no regrets."

Brown had captured the attention of the entire courtroom
with his questioning. Judge Parker, who had been reading a
newspaper at the start of the day's testimony, began to focus on
Brown, this uneducated farmer who was conducting himself in
the courtroom with the skills of a graduate from Harvard University Law School.

Brown wanted additional witnesses to be called, but they
were not in court. Judge Parker, anxious to bring the trial to a
close, recommended that Brown rest his case. Brown was furious
at the judge's suggestion, and he delivered to the court a lecture
concerning the fairness of his trial:

> May it please the court, I discover that, notwithstanding
> all the assertions that I would receive a fair trial, nothing
> like a fair trial is to be given to me, as it would seem. I

gave the names as soon as I could get them, of the persons I wished to have called as witnesses, and was assured that they would be subpoenaed [summoned to court]. I wrote down a memorandum to that effect, saying where those parties were, but it appears that they have not been subpoenaed, so far as I can learn. And now I ask, if I am to have anything at all deserving the name and shadow of a fair trial, that this proceeding be deferred until tomorrow morning; for I have no counsel, as I have before stated, in whom I feel that I can rely, but I am in hopes counsel may arrive who will see that I get the witnesses necessary for my defense.

Brown went on to explain that his money had been confiscated and that he could not adequately pay for legal counsel without it. He concluded his speech by asking for a one-day delay in the trial.

New Attorneys

After hearing that oration, Brown's court-appointed lawyers, realizing that their efforts were not appreciated, resigned from the case, and young Hoyt was left alone as Brown's defense attorney. Hoyt immediately asked for a delay so that he might prepare a proper defense. Prosecutor Hunter opposed any delay. He was willing to grant the court the substance of Brown's defense—that he had not harmed any hostages and that the citizens of Harpers Ferry had not properly respected Brown's flags of truce. Judge Parker, acknowledging that Brown was entitled to call additional witnesses, agreed to adjourn for the day, but he informed Brown that the trial would continue the next day, Saturday, October 29.

The next morning, two defense attorneys arrived in Charles Town to defend Brown, Samuel Chilton of Massachusetts and Hiram Griswold of Ohio, both sent and paid for by Brown's abolitionist friends. They had less than one day to prepare Brown's defense, and they decided to stick with the strategy that Brown had developed in the courtroom the previous day. So on the trial's fourth day, Brown's new lawyers brought other witnesses

TRIALS FOR BROWN'S MEN

Several of John Brown's Harpers Ferry invaders were tried during the days following Brown's sentencing. On November 2, immediately after Brown was sentenced by Judge Parker, Edwin Coppoc was tried and convicted in a single day. A few days later, Shields Green and John Copeland, two of Brown's African American recruits, were tried separately and each found guilty. The next day, John Cook, who had escaped from Harpers Ferry and had been captured in Pennsylvania a week later, was also tried and convicted. After Cook's trial, Judge Parker summoned all four men to court for sentencing. He sentenced them to die on the gallows on December 16, 1859, two weeks after the execution of their ringleader, John Brown.

The trials of two more raiders, Albert Hazlett, who had also escaped and had been apprehended in Pennsylvania, and Aaron Stevens, were delayed until February. Unlike the other Harpers Ferry raiders, these two men were arraigned on federal charges and tried in a federal court. But the results were similar. Both men were found guilty and sentenced to hang.

Five of Brown's men, including his son Owen, escaped from Harpers Ferry and were never caught.

to the stand to testify that Brown had not harmed his hostages in any way, that he had hoped not to spill the blood of innocent townspeople during his Harpers Ferry raid, and that he and his men had fired gunshots only in self-defense.

The prosecution wished to conclude the trial by Saturday night, but testimony continued into the early evening, at which time Judge Parker called for a recess until Monday morning, when the prosecution and defense would present their final arguments.

Closing Arguments

On Sunday Brown's three lawyers visited his jail cell to discuss strategy. Griswold and Chilton suggested that Brown consider a plea bargain, pleading guilty to a less serious charge with the hope of avoiding execution as a punishment. But Brown rejected that strategy. "I am almost fully persuaded that I am worth more to hang than for any other purpose," he stated.

On Monday morning Brown returned to court, and the defense and prosecution presented their final summary arguments to the jury. Griswold made an eloquent plea on Brown's behalf. He asserted that Brown had taken only temporary possession of the armory buildings, that Brown was not "levying war against the state of Virginia." He argued that Brown's Provisional Constitution and Ordinances was not a treasonous document but merely a set of rules like those "governing a military company or a debating society." Griswold went on to praise Brown as "a man of indomitable will, of sleepless energy, of purpose, possessed of a perseverance that turns back from no difficulty, and endowed with a constitution that will endure and overcome anything." Griswold concluded that Brown was guilty only of trying to free slaves, "with interfering with that species of property."

Hunter summarized for the prosecution. He argued that Brown's "provisional government was a real thing, and no debating society, as his counsel would have us believe." According to Hunter, Brown's "purposes were well matured and he and his party declared that there were thousands in the North ready to join him." Brown had intended to "usurp the government, manumit [free] our slaves, confiscate the property of slaveholders, . . . take possession of the Commonwealth." Hunter advised the jury to "acquit the prisoner if you can—but if justice requires you by your verdict to take his life, stand by that column uprightly, but strongly, and let retributive justice, if he is guilty, send him before that Maker who will settle the question forever and ever."

The Verdict

The jury took just forty-five minutes to decide on a verdict of guilty, on all charges. According to one newspaper account, Brown stood to face Judge Parker and receive the verdict as "a man of indomitable will and iron nerves, all collected and unmoved, even while the verdict that consigned him to an ignominious doom was pronounced upon him."

Brown was brought back to court two days later, on November 2, for sentencing. Before Judge Parker delivered Brown his sentence, he asked the prisoner if he had anything else to say. Brown delivered a speech that would be recorded by reporters and printed in newspapers all over America in the following days. He began by denying all charges but one—"the design on my part to free the slaves." He asserted that if he had tried to interfere "in behalf of the rich, the powerful, the intelligent, the so-called great, or in behalf of any of their friends," his actions would have been deemed "all right." He suggested that the court acknowledges "the law of God" and the Bible, which "teaches me further, to 'remember them that are in bonds, as

GOVERNOR WISE PLOTS TO INVADE HARPERS FERRY

The man most responsible for John Brown's swift trial after the Harpers Ferry raid was Virginia governor Henry Wise. He judged Brown's actions to be both sinful and treasonous and wanted to see him hang without delay after a quick trial.

Ironically, eighteen months after Brown's raid on Harpers Ferry, Wise would conspire to attempt a similar endeavor. After the election of Abraham Lincoln as president of the United States in November 1860, the political leaders of several Southern states threatened to secede from the Union in protest. Henry Wise, now an ex-governor, was among the most vocal secessionists, calling on Virginians to divorce themselves from the nation ruled by the abolitionist Lincoln and his supporters. In April 1861 Virginia did follow the lead of several other Southern states and voted to withdraw from the Union. At the convention at which Virginia voted to secede, Wise made one of the most persuasive prosecession speeches.

The day before the Virginia secession convention, Wise had met with several Virginia militia commanders and plotted to invade the federal armory at Harpers Ferry and seize the weapons there for use in the inevitable war between the Southern states that had seceded and the United States. Unfortunately for Wise, the federal troops guarding the weaponry and weapon factories at Harpers Ferry anticipated such a move and burned much of the Harpers Ferry weapons works that Brown had seized eighteen months earlier. Virginia militiamen invaded Harpers Ferry on the day after Virginia seceded from the Union, only to find that the federal troops had destroyed most of the weapons-production materials and fled town. The Virginia militia was able to salvage some machinery, which was shipped to Richmond, where it could be more easily guarded.

During the Civil War, Wise served as a general in the army of the Confederate States of America. Having no substantial military experience before the Civil War began, General Wise did not distinguish himself on the battlefield during the conflict.

John Brown is led from the courtroom after he is sentenced to hang.

bound with them.' I endeavored to act up to that instruction." He stated that if his blood must be mingled "with the blood of millions in this slave country whose rights are disregarded by wicked, cruel, and unjust enactments, . . . so let it be done."

Judge Parker listened patiently, then delivered the sentence: John Brown would hang from the gallows until dead one month hence, on December 2.

Hearing the sentence, one courtroom spectator began to applaud. When no one joined in the applause, the man stopped and walked out of the courthouse. The courtroom was absolutely silent when Brown was led back to his jail cell.

But Judge Parker had given Brown a one-month reprieve. He would have thirty days to continue to carry his gospel of anti-slavery to the American people. The entire country had been watching the trial; Americans across the continent had followed the saga of John Brown every day in their daily newspapers. And almost everyone—Northerner and Southerner, slaveholder and abolitionist—had formed an opinion about John Brown.

Chapter 4

The Public Reaction

A LMOST ALL AMERICANS CAPABLE of reading a newspaper closely followed the trial of John Brown and formed an opinion on his Harpers Ferry raid. To many Americans, particularly those living in the slaveholding South, Brown was an evil man, a murderer, who confiscated federal property in an attempt to overthrow the government and who attempted to ruin the South's agricultural economy by liberating the slaves. To many abolitionists, however, Brown was a hero, even a saint, who was doing God's work by trying to end slavery in America. Other Americans who opposed slavery sympathized with Brown's objective—to free the slaves—but condemned his methods; they believed that slavery should be curtailed and eliminated through legal means, not by violent rebellion. The debate on John Brown engaged the entire nation and took place in town squares, on city streets, in the editorial pages of dozens of newspapers, and even in the halls of Congress.

The Southern Response

The South's political leaders strongly condemned Brown. Soon after Brown's arrest, several proslavery Southern Democrats in Congress—Senator Jefferson Davis of Mississippi, Senator James Mason of Virginia, Senator James Chesnut of South Carolina, among others—and a few of their Democratic allies in the North met with President James Buchanan and demanded a special congressional investigation of the Harpers Ferry raid. They believed that Brown and his twenty-one Harpers Ferry

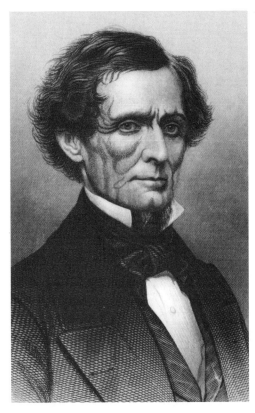

Mississippi senator Jefferson Davis (pictured) demanded further inquiry into the John Brown case, believing that Brown had been part of a conspiracy.

invaders were not acting alone; the South's political leaders maintained that Brown had the support of abolitionists throughout the United States, who were plotting to use violent means to attain their objective. These angry Southerners in Congress wanted to force the political leaders of the North who had identified themselves as abolitionists—men like Governor Salmon Chase of Ohio, Senator Charles Sumner of Massachusetts, and Senator William Seward of New York—to answer questions under oath about their support for Brown and his Harpers Ferry escapade. The South's political leaders wanted all of Brown's supporters tried and punished properly as conspirators in his plan to start a slave rebellion.

The Southern press was even more angry than the South's politicians. Editorials in Southern newspapers condemned Brown as an agent of Satan, a treasonous murderer who wished to destroy Southern society. Typical of these biting editorials was one that appeared in the *Register*, published in Mobile, Alabama. "The ark of covenant has been desecrated," asserted an editorial in the *Register*. "For the first time the soil of the South has been invaded and its blood has been shed upon its own soil by armed abolitionists." The *Patriot*, published in Albany, Georgia, condemned Brown as a "notorious old thief and murderer" who deserved to be quickly hanged for his offenses.

Many Southerners believed that Brown's Harpers Ferry raid would lead to a civil war between the Northern and Southern states. They believed that Brown was certainly backed by the abolitionist forces in the North and that Brown's Harpers Ferry raid was actually an organized attempt by the North to exterminate slavery through a rebellion that would surely lead to war. The South reasoned that the era of compromise between the North and South on the issue of slavery was over. The warfare that developed in Kansas a few years earlier had taken place in a remote U.S. territory on the western frontier, but Brown's raid had taken place in Virginia, the heart of Southern society. Proslavery Southerners predicted that a bloody war between the North and South over slavery was on the horizon. The *Enquirer* of Richmond, Virginia, asserted that "the Harpers Ferry invasion has advanced the cause of Disunion more than any other event that has happened since the formation of the Government." *De Bow's Review*, a Southern journal, stated that the North had "sanctioned and applauded

Southern political leaders wanted to question Northern abolitionists, including Ohio governor Salmon Chase (pictured), about their possible connections to John Brown.

A Southern planter arms his slaves to safeguard against an armed invasion from the North. Southern citizens were afraid of further rebellion in the aftermath of the John Brown trial.

theft, murder, treason" and "has shed Southern Blood on Southern soil! There is—there can be no peace!"

Indeed, the South began to prepare for war. Throughout the South, the state militias were called to duty and ordered to prepare for a Northern invasion or a slave rebellion. Even though Brown had completely failed at Harpers Ferry, Southerners believed that other abolitionists would follow Brown's lead and organize slave rebellions throughout the South. Among the documents seized in Brown's carpetbag were various maps of Southern counties with large slave populations, places where Brown had hoped to spread his slave rebellion as it gained momentum after a victory at Harpers Ferry. The residents of these counties prepared for war. Many slave owners began to police their slaves more closely and punish them more severely for any unruly behavior.

Reaction in the North

The North did not speak with one voice on Brown's Harpers Ferry invasion. To many abolitionists, Brown was surely a hero. In Concord, Massachusetts, Ralph Waldo Emerson and Henry David Thoreau, two of the nation's most eloquent abolitionist

THOREAU'S PLEA FOR JOHN BROWN

John Brown had many defenders among America's literary men and women, but none spoke or wrote more eloquently about him than Henry David Thoreau, the essayist and orator from Concord, Massachusetts.

In 1859 Thoreau was not well known outside the Concord and Boston literary communities. In 1845 he had embarked on a two-year experiment by living a life of simplicity in a small cabin at Walden Pond, near Concord. Thoreau recorded his experiences in a remarkable volume titled *Walden*, a book not widely read during Thoreau's lifetime but destined to become an American classic. In 1849, after spending a night in prison for refusing to pay his taxes, Thoreau wrote an essay titled "Resistance to Civil Government." The essay, later retitled "Civil Disobedience," asserted that individuals had a right to break laws that they considered unjust—and Thoreau would

Henry David Thoreau

judge any law protecting slavery as an unjust law. Like *Walden*, "Civil Disobedience" was not widely read or appreciated during Thoreau's lifetime, but it would become one of the most influential literary texts penned by an American writer.

After the passage of the Fugitive Slave Law in 1850, Thoreau became an avid spokesman for the abolitionist cause. He railed against the institution of slavery in "Slavery in Massachusetts" and in other lectures and essays. Not surprisingly, he came to Brown's defense after the failed raid on Harpers Ferry. As far as Thoreau was concerned, Brown had a right to break the law—to seize federal property, to free slaves, even to use violence to achieve his goals—because slavery was unjust.

During Brown's trial, Thoreau delivered "A Plea for Captain John Brown" at the Concord Lyceum and in Boston and Worcester as well. Thoreau saluted Brown as a man who "gave his life to the cause of the oppressed." Thoreau asserted that Brown had "a perfect right to interfere by force with the slaveholder, in order to rescue the slave," that "for once the Sharpe's rifles and the revolvers were employed in a righteous cause. The tools were in the hands of one who could use them." Thoreau knew that no plea from the Concord Lyceum could save Brown's life. "I am here to plead his cause with you," declared Thoreau. "I plead not for his life, but for his character—his immortal life; and so it becomes your cause wholly and is not his in the least."

voices, defended Brown and his methods. In one of his lectures, Emerson praised Brown as "that new saint, than whom none purer or more brave was ever led by love of men into conflict and death,—the new saint awaiting his martyrdom, and who, if he shall suffer, will make the gallows glorious like the cross." Thoreau delivered a lecture titled "A Plea for Captain John Brown" in Concord, Boston, and Worcester, Massachusetts. Thoreau called Brown a man who moved "against the legions of Slavery, in obedience to an infinitely higher command." Thoreau asserted, "I would rather see a statue of Captain Brown in the Massachusetts State-House yard, than that of any other man whom I know."

Other literary men and women echoed the views of Emerson and Thoreau. The poet Henry Wadsworth Longfellow pointed to the day of Brown's scheduled execution as "a great day in our history; the date of a new Revolution,—quite as needed as the old one." Ringing defenses of Brown also came from the pens and voices of Harriet Beecher Stowe, William Lloyd Garrison, and other writers committed to the abolitionist cause.

But not all antislavery Northerners supported Brown. Some prominent members of the newly formed Republican Party, a

Poet and essayist Ralph Waldo Emerson praised John Brown for his activities, comparing him to a martyred saint.

THE REPUBLICAN PARTY

The Republican Party was formed in 1854, when the Whig Party fell into disunion, mainly over the issue of slavery. Immediately afterward, antislavery Whigs began meeting in various Northern states to discuss their concerns, and out of these meetings came a new national party dedicated to opposing the spread of slavery.

The new political party attracted a wide range of antislavery politicians and supporters. Some, like William Seward of New York, were strong abolitionists who favored either an immediate or gradual end to American slavery. Southern Democrats labeled these Republicans as the "Black Republicans" because of their identification with the issue of slavery. Other Republicans, like Abraham Lincoln of Illinois, were opposed to slavery but did not call for its abolition; they would tolerate slavery where it already existed, but they opposed any expansion of slavery into the United States territories, such as Kansas and Nebraska.

In the election of 1856, the Republicans put forth their first presidential candidate, John Frémont of California, in a three-party race against James Buchanan of the Democratic Party and Millard Fillmore of the American Party. Frémont finished second, receiving 114 electoral votes to Buchanan's 174.

In 1860 the Republicans selected Lincoln as their candidate at their national convention in Chicago. The Democrats split into two factions. Northern Democrats put forward Senator Stephen Douglas, who had beaten Lincoln for an Illinois senate seat two years earlier; and Southern Democrats nominated Vice President John Breckenridge of Kentucky as their candidate. The remaining Whigs nominated Senator John Bell of Tennessee. In the election, Lincoln, carrying virtually the entire North, captured 180 electoral votes to 72 for Breckenridge, 39 for Bell, and 12 for Douglas. In March 1861 Lincoln became president, after which eleven Southern states seceded from the Union.

---

party committed to curtailing the spread of American slavery, wished to distance themselves from Brown and his Harpers Ferry raid. Some Republican leaders feared that Brown would be closely linked to the Republican leadership and that the party would be accused of conspiring with Brown to overthrow the government. Abraham Lincoln, a Republican leader who in 1859 was beginning to gain national attention, claimed that "John Brown was no Republican" and that Republicans were not involved in his activities at Harpers Ferry. Nonetheless, Republicans continued to be viewed with suspicion by their Southern Democratic colleagues in Congress.

Many antislavery Americans sympathized with Brown's motives and goals—they, too, wished to put an end to American slavery—but condemned his methods. Many believed that Brown, by trying to ignite a violent revolution, had gone too far in his effort to free the slaves. These individuals felt that the battle against slavery should be conducted through the proper legal channels—by passing antislavery legislation, for example. Many Americans who opposed slavery also opposed Brown's use of violence to achieve his objective. Some actually questioned Brown's sanity. Even William Lloyd Garrison's antislavery newspaper, the *Liberator*, called Brown's Harpers Ferry insurrection "a misguided, wild, and apparently insane—effort."

The African American Community Responds

To most African Americans, John Brown was a hero, a Moses who had attempted to lead black people out of bondage to the promised land of freedom. After Brown's capture and throughout his trial, spirited defenses of Brown rang from the editorial pages of African American newspapers and from the pulpits of African American churches.

Typical of the effort by African Americans to canonize Brown was a commentary published in the *Cleveland Plain Dealer* by Charles Langston, an African American abolitionist leader from Ohio. Langston, who earlier in 1859 had served a twenty-day jail sentence for assisting a runaway slave, stated that Brown

> was engaged in no vile, base, sordid, malicious or selfish enterprise. His aims and ends were lofty, noble, generous, benevolent, humane and Godlike. His actions were in perfect harmony with, and resulted from the teaching of the Bible, of our Revolutionary fathers and of every true and faithful anti-slavery man in this country and the world.

According to Langston, Brown "went to Virginia to aid the afflicted and the helpless, to assist the weak and to relieve the

OTHER VOICES FROM HARPERS FERRY

John Brown was not the only one of the Harpers Ferry raiders to use his time in captivity as an opportunity to preach the antislavery gospel. Several of Brown's recruits were men with a fluent command of the English language. Their letters and statements to the court were printed in the nation's newspapers and read by thousands of Americans.

On December 10, 1859, John Anthony Copeland, one of Brown's African American recruits, while awaiting his execution, defended his actions in a moving letter to his brother:

> It was a sense of the wrongs which we have suffered that prompted the noble but unfortunate Captain Brown and his associates to attempt to give freedom to a small number, at least, of those who are now held by cruel and unjust laws, and by no less cruel and unjust men. To this freedom they were entitled by every known principle of justice and humanity, and for the enjoyment of it God created them. And now, dear brother, could I die in a more noble cause? Could I, brother, die in a manner and for a cause which would induce true and honest men more to honor me, and the angels more readily to receive me to their happy home of everlasting joy above?

Copeland had attended Oberlin College in Ohio and had met Brown while working for the Oberlin Anti-Slavery Society.

poor and needy"; Brown's actions were "only the results of his faithfulness to the plain teaching of the word of God."

A few weeks after Brown's trial, a group of African American women from New York wrote a letter to Brown's wife, Mary, at the Brown family farm in North Elba, New York. In their letter, these women called Brown "our honored and dearly-loved brother" who is "dear to our God as the apple of his eye." They promised Mary Brown to "organize in every Free State, and in every colored church, a band of sisters, to collect our weekly pence, and pour it lovingly into your lap."

The Reaction of Frederick Douglass

Surprisingly, however, the nation's most eloquent African American abolitionist, Frederick Douglass, attempted to separate himself from Brown and his actions at Harpers Ferry. The Virginia authorities who prosecuted Brown knew that he had worked closely with Douglass in the past, and letters from Douglass were found in Brown's carpetbag at the time of Brown's arrest. Douglass was worried that he would be indicted as one of Brown's conspirators. Indeed, Brown had attempted to recruit Douglass for the Harpers Ferry raid, but Douglass, convinced that Brown was sure to fail, had decided not to join him.

Douglass was in Canada at the time of Brown's arrest and trial. Douglass had heard that Governor Henry Wise of Virginia had petitioned President Buchanan to have Douglass arrested and that federal marshals had visited his home in Rochester, New York, to interview him about Harpers Ferry. During Brown's trial Douglass, from Canada, penned a letter to the editor of the *Rochester Democrat*, a letter that was later reprinted in *Douglass Monthly*. In the letter, Douglass tried to protect himself by disassociating himself from Brown, yet he tried not to directly criticize Brown's actions. "The taking of Harpers Ferry was a measure never encouraged by my word or by my vote, at any time or place," insisted Douglass. "My field of labor for the abolition of Slavery has not extended to an attack upon the United States Arsenal." Douglass stated, however, that he was "ever ready to write, speak, publish, organize, combine, and even to conspire against Slavery" and that "it can never be wrong for the imbrutted [made brutish] and whip-scarred slaves, or their friends, to hunt, harass, and even strike down the traffickers in human flesh." In the letter, Douglass referred to Brown as "the noble old hero whose right hand has shaken the foundation of the American Union, and whose ghost will haunt the bedchambers of all the born and unborn slaveholders of Virginia through their generations, filling them with alarm and consternation!"

After Brown's trial, Douglass departed for England, where he had planned a speaking tour. He tried to make clear to his followers that he had planned his trip overseas long before Brown had invaded Harpers Ferry, that he was not leaving the country to avoid questioning about Brown. Nonetheless, the scheduled trip abroad enabled Douglass to absent himself from the United States as the South's anger over Brown reached its highest point.

Douglass was not the only one of Brown's supporters who feared for his own safety after Brown's failure at Harpers Ferry and his subsequent arrest. The members of Brown's Secret Six saw themselves as particularly vulnerable. They had known of the Harpers Ferry raid months in advance. They had raised money for Brown's endeavor, sent him weapons, and provided him with recruits. The letters of the members of the Secret Six were found by the Harpers Ferry sheriff at the Kennedy farmhouse after Brown was taken captive. These men could surely be arrested and charged with conspiring with Brown to commit murder and treason, crimes punishable by long prison sentences, even execution.

Running for Cover

Franklin Sanborn, the teacher from Concord, fled to Canada shortly after Brown's arrest. He destroyed all of Brown's letters that he still had in his possession, lest they be seized and used as evidence against himself. Sanborn did return to Concord for a short time and conspired with other Brown supporters on one of the plans to rescue Brown from his Charles Town prison cell. But Sanborn later fled again to Canada when the Senate began its investigation of the Harpers Ferry raid.

Samuel Howe and George Luther Stearns also fled to Canada. From Canada, Howe wrote a statement that was printed in the *New York Tribune*. In that statement, Howe disavowed any knowledge of Brown's Harpers Ferry enterprise, calling it "a mystery and a marvel."

Theodore Parker, the abolitionist clergyman, was living in Rome at the time of the Harpers Ferry ordeal, suffering from an illness that would take his life within the year, so he feared little for his own safety. But Gerrit Smith, the wealthy landowner from New York, became greatly alarmed after Brown's arrest. The New York newspapers printed the texts of some of Smith's letters that were found among Brown's belongings, and Smith became very fearful that he would be immediately arrested. His fear became more pronounced after Brown was sentenced to death. Smith was unable to sleep and began imagining that federal agents were descending upon his home to take him into custody. Thinking that Smith was going mad, his friends had him committed to the State Asylum for the Insane in Utica, New York, where he remained for several weeks. When Smith returned home, he denied any knowledge of Brown's plans for invading Harpers Ferry.

Of the Secret Six, only Thomas Wentworth Higginson, the Boston writer and editor, faced his accusers. He admitted publicly that he had supported Brown, and he praised Brown and his actions in his lectures and his writings. Rather than flee the country, Higginson began to work on a

Of Brown's allies, only Thomas Wentworth Higginson publicly supported Brown's actions.

plan to rescue Brown from the gallows. Higginson traveled to North Elba, New York, to visit Mary Brown and to acquaint her with the plot to spring Brown free. Nonetheless, Higginson was never indicted for conspiring with Brown.

The First Volley in a Civil War

Some of the personal friends and family members of Brown and his fellow captives also grew concerned for themselves during and after Brown's trial. But it became clear that the Southerners set on uprooting a Harpers Ferry conspiracy were more interested in entrapping well-known abolitionist leaders, men like Frederick Douglass and William Lloyd Garrison, and leading Republican politicians. If these men could be indicted, tried, and found guilty of conspiracy, Southerners would be confirmed in their belief that Brown's invasion of Harpers Ferry was only the starting point for a slave rebellion and a subsequent civil war designed to abolish slavery and destroy the South.

JOHN BROWN'S MOST STEADFAST DEFENDER: THOMAS WENTWORTH HIGGINSON

Many of John Brown's supporters disassociated themselves from Brown after his raid at Harpers Ferry ended in failure. Some published statements asserting that though they supported the abolitionist cause, they knew nothing of his activities at Harpers Ferry. A few fled to Canada, where they would be safe from prosecution by federal authorities in the United States. Thomas Wentworth Higginson neither fled nor disavowed knowledge of Brown's actions.

The Massachusetts-born Higginson was trained as a minister but left the clergy as a young man to devote himself to literature. During the 1850s he worked as an editor, published essays on a wide variety of topics, and dedicated himself to the abolitionist cause. He became one of the Secret Six who helped plan and finance Brown's Harpers Ferry raid—and he would become the only member of that group not to go into hiding after Brown's raid failed. After Brown's arrest, Higginson remained in Boston, defying Governor Henry Wise of Virginia to come forward to arrest him. Higginson also spearheaded a group of prominent Boston abolitionists in a plot to rescue Brown from the gallows, though their plan was never put into action.

After Brown's death, Higginson continued working for the abolitionist cause. Shortly after the Civil War began, he was commissioned as an officer in the Union army. In 1863 Higginson was given command of a regiment of African American soldiers, the First South Carolina Volunteers, which consisted entirely of ex-slaves. President Abraham Lincoln had come under criticism by some for allowing ex-slaves to join the Union army because, it was widely believed, African American soldiers would be difficult to train and would not perform bravely in combat. Higginson proved those charges to be without foundation by developing the First South Carolina Volunteers into a crack regiment that performed effectively on the battlefield. After the war, Higginson recorded his experiences with the First South Carolina Volunteers in a stimulating memoir, *Army Life in a Black Regiment.*

In 1862 Higginson had begun a long correspondence with a very private young poet from Amherst, Massachusetts, named Emily Dickinson. Dickinson wrote hundreds of poems but attempted to publish none of them. Higginson urged Dickinson to send him samples of her poetry, which he recognized as the work of a genius. After Dickinson's death in 1886, Higginson supervised the publication of a comprehensive volume of her poetry. His judgment on the merit of her work was sound. Dickinson is now regarded as one of America's finest poets.

During his lifetime, Higginson also devoted himself to the cause of women's rights. He died in 1911, after a life of eighty-eight years and many accomplishments.

To Brown's defenders, and to those who criticized his methods yet supported his goal of ending slavery, the Harpers Ferry raid was a warning signal to the South that the North had tolerated slavery long enough, that antislavery individuals were ready to fight and die to see slavery eradicated from the United States. To many Americans, the war to end American slavery had begun at Harpers Ferry.

As Brown lay in his jail cell awaiting execution, Americans continued to debate his actions and the cause for which he was about to give his life. The tone of that discussion became more and more angry. The time for respectful debate and compromise on the issue of slavery seemed to have passed; the time for armed conflict seemed to be approaching.

Chapter 5

The Sentence

O N NOVEMBER 2, 1859, Judge Richard Parker sentenced John Brown to hang from the gallows in thirty days. Hence, Brown would have one month to put his personal affairs in order before he would die, one month to continue to spread his anti-slavery gospel to a nation that was paying close attention to what was happening in Charles Town, Virginia. Brown would use the short time allotted to him very well—by writing letters, by preaching to anyone who would listen and record his words, by saying good-bye to loved ones—and he would face death with a dignity that would impress even his political opponents and would keep his name in America's memory long after his corpse was laid to rest in North Elba, New York.

The Question of Brown's Sanity

Shortly after Brown was sentenced to death, his lawyers began an effort to save his life. Their plan was to make the case that Brown was insane, a charge that Brown had refuted at his trial. If he was certified as insane, Brown could not be held legally responsible for his actions at Harpers Ferry. Instead of being executed, Brown, if labeled insane, would be committed to an insane asylum for the rest of his life.

George Hoyt, one of Brown's lawyers, traveled to Ohio, where he collected from Brown's friends and family members sworn affidavits that maintained that insanity ran in Brown's family, on his mother's side. Some of the affidavits also asserted that Brown himself had suffered fits of insanity during his lifetime. "I have known John Brown for 15 years and never saw any business transaction conducted by him which indicated a Sane mind—excepting while engaged in Summit County in growing sheep & wool," asserted one affidavit. One of Brown's friends from Akron, Ohio, gave as evidence of his insanity Brown's claim that he was an instrument in the hands of God to free the slaves.

Historians continue to debate the question of Brown's sanity. Certainly he was a fanatic—fanatically devoted to and obsessed with his cause: ending American slavery. And certainly his plan for achieving his goal was rather far-fetched. Rational men like Frederick Douglass foresaw that the Harpers Ferry raid was a foolish enterprise that would end in certain disaster. But labeling Brown as insane would deem it necessary to label the thousands of other devoted abolitionists across the United States insane as well. As the *Boston Post* commented on the issue, if Brown were a lunatic, "then one-fourth of the people of Massachusetts are madmen." Henry David Thoreau also took up the question of Brown's sanity in his essay "A Plea for Captain John Brown," refuting those who gave as evidence of Brown's insanity his claim that he was appointed by God to free the slaves:

> Newspaper editors argue that it is a proof of his *insanity* that he thought he was appointed to do this work which he did. . . . They talk as if it were impossible that a man could be "divinely appointed" in these days to do any work whatever; as if vows and religion were out of date as connected with any man's daily work,—as if the agent to abolish Slavery could only be somebody appointed by the President, or by some political party.

Virginia governor Henry Wise, the man most responsible for prosecuting Brown, also commented on Brown's sanity. "They are themselves mistaken who take him to be a madman," reported Governor Wise after interviewing Brown. "He is cool, collected, and indomitable. . . . And he inspired me with great trust in his integrity as a man of truth. He is fanatic, vain, and garrulous, but firm, truthful, and intelligent."

Virginia governor Henry Wise (pictured) did not believe that John Brown was insane, calling him "firm, truthful, and intelligent."

Brown's comments during and after his trial support Governor Wise's evaluation. Brown's eloquent courtroom statements and the contents of letters that he wrote while in jail do not suggest that he was insane. He knew precisely what he had tried to achieve at Harpers Ferry; he was fully aware at all times during his trial; and he had a keen insight into what his death would mean for the abolitionist cause. Historian Stephen B. Oates makes the following comment on the question of Brown's sanity in a biography of Brown:

> Yet to dismiss Brown as an "insane" man is to ignore the tremendous sympathy he felt for the suffering of the black man in the United States; it is to disregard the fact that at a time when most Northerners and almost all Southerners were racists who wanted to keep the Negro at the bottom of society, John Brown was able to treat America's "poor despised Africans" as fellow human beings. And to label him a "maniac" out of touch with "reality" is to ignore the piercing insight he had into what his raid—whether it succeeded or whether it failed—would do to sectional tensions that already existed between North and South.

Oates also points out that the main evidence used to demonstrate Brown's insanity, the affidavits signed by Brown's family members and friends, is highly suspect. The persons who signed those affidavits were determined to save Brown's life; these people believed that statements alleging Brown's insanity would spare him from the gallows.

SUPPORT FROM ABROAD

The saga of John Brown was closely followed not only in the United States but in Europe as well. From abroad came support from Victor Hugo, the French author, and Karl Marx, the German philosopher and economist. In a letter that appeared in the *London Daily News*, the *Northern Bee* of St. Petersburg, Russia, and the *New York Tribune*, Hugo depicted Brown as a martyr, "the champion of Christ." Hugo questioned the fairness of Brown's trial and concluded his statement with a warning for America:

> Such things cannot be done with impunity in the face of the civilized world. The universal conscience of humanity is an ever watchful eye. Let the judges of Charlestown and Hunter and the slaveholding jurors and the whole population of Virginia, ponder on it well; they are watched!

In the words of Marx, writing to his friend Friedrich Engels, one of "the biggest things . . . happening in the world today" was "the movement of the slaves in America, started by the death of John Brown."

From England, as well, came voices of protest over the execution of John Brown. The international antislavery community had carefully followed Brown's ordeal and reacted with outrage when its hero was put to death.

Governor Wise rejected Hoyt's insanity appeal. Brown, too, rejected any effort to label him insane. Brown also rejected any plan to rescue him from the gallows, though the men who plotted Brown's escape had already come to the sad conclusion that a rescue attempt would not likely be successful. Brown's prison cell was being closely guarded by hundreds of Virginia militiamen and by federal troops under the command of Colonel Robert E. Lee. "Let them hang me," Brown wrote in a letter to his brother Jeremiah. "I am worth inconceivably more to *hang* than for any other purpose."

Final Letters

So Brown waited patiently for his execution day to arrive. Confined to a small jail cell, he had little to do to pass the time. He read from the Bible and spent much time during the final month of his life writing letters, answering the many letters that arrived at his prison cell from friends, supporters, family members, and complete strangers who wished to offer Brown their sympathy. Brown's letters, some of which have survived, reflect a man at peace with himself, facing death with great courage and dignity.

In his first letter to his wife after being taken captive, Brown briefly recounted the Harpers Ferry raid and provided details about the deaths and wounds of his recruits. When he completed the text of the letter, he had not yet been sentenced. By the time Brown was ready to mail the letter, however, he had already been ordered to hang by Judge Parker. So Brown added a postscript at the end of the letter: "Nov. 2nd I was sentenced to be hanged on Dec. 2nd next. Do not grieve on my account. I am still quite cheerful. God bless you all." Brown expressed the same cheerful acceptance of death in a letter that he penned to a Quaker woman who had written to say that she was praying for Brown every day: "I wish you could know with what cheerfulness I am now wielding the 'sword of the spirit.' I bless God that it proves mighty to the pulling down of strongholds."

Brown accepted his coming death as the will of God. He wrote to a cousin:

> The scaffold has but few terrors for me. God has often covered my head in the day of battle and granted me many times deliverances that were almost so miraculous I can scarce realize their truth; and now, when it seems quite certain he intends to use me in a *different way*, shall I not most cheerfully go?

Similarly, Brown stated in a letter to one of his former teachers, "I tell you that I am 'joyfull in all my tribulations': that I do not feel condemned of Him whose judgment is just; nor of my own conscience. Nor do I feel degraded by my imprisonment, my chains or prospects of the Gallows." On November 27, five days before his scheduled execution, Brown wrote his sisters that he was weeping tears of joy and gratitude that God had chosen this course for him.

On November 30, two days before his execution, Brown composed a letter to his wife, Mary. In it, he instructed Mary on how to raise his youngest daughters, who still lived at home with her. He asked Mary to be certain that his daughters grew up loving God and that they used the Bible as their "dayly & Nightly study." He urged that his daughters be taught to love their family members and abhor slavery "with *undying hatred*." He concluded his letter by stating that he was certain that his "seeming *disaster*" would "ultimately result in the most *glorious success*," and he looked forward with confidence "in the certain & near approach of a *bright Morning; & a glorious day*."

A Visit from Mary

But Brown would have the opportunity to speak directly to his beloved wife, Mary, once more before his appointment at the gallows. In late November, Brown's friend and supporter Thomas Wentworth Higginson had gone to the Brown farm in North Elba, New York, to arrange for Mary to visit her husband before his execution.

Mary arrived in Charles Town, Virginia, by train on the afternoon of December 1, the day before Brown was scheduled to be hanged. Mary was searched by the jailer's wife for weapons or poison before being allowed to see her husband. Brown's chains were removed for the visit, and he was allowed to leave his cell, under guard, to meet with his wife in the jailer's living quarters. There they spoke for a few hours and enjoyed a final meal together.

Brown assured Mary that he was cheerfully looking forward to his moment on the gallows, that he was assured that his execution would be good for the abolitionist cause in the long run. He delivered to Mary a copy of his will and made suggestions regarding his burial. When it was time for Mary to leave, Brown asked that she be allowed to stay the night. Brown's guards told him that his request could not be granted; Mary would have to be taken to Harpers Ferry that night, where she would wait for his body. Mary departed, and Brown was left alone to face the last evening of his life.

The Hanging

Brown woke at dawn on the last day of his life. He read his favorite Bible passages and composed a final note to Mary, which

In this romanticized illustration, slaves wait to speak with John Brown as he is escorted from prison to his execution in Charles Town, Virginia.

included an inscription for his tombstone. Later in the morning, past ten o'clock, the jailer and guards entered his cell to lead him away. Brown gave his Bible to one of the guards and presented his silver watch to John Avis, the jailer who had treated Brown kindly during the final weeks of his life. As he exited the jail, Brown passed the cells of his fellow captives and bade them farewell. He urged them to show courage when their day at the gallows arrived. But Brown completely ignored the cell of Albert

Hazlett, one of his raiders who had been captured in Pennsylvania several days after the Harpers Ferry raid. Brown was hoping that Hazlett would not be positively identified as one of his recruits, so Brown did not want to let on in front of his jailers that he knew Hazlett.

As Brown left the prison compound, he saw hundreds of troops in formation on the streets of Charles Town. Governor Wise still expected Brown's supporters to stage some kind of rescue attempt, and he had prepared well for that possibility. Brown was directed to a wagon that carried his coffin, and he was ordered to sit atop the casket for his ride to the gallows. As he boarded the wagon, Brown, still the preacher, handed a short written message to one of the guards:

Charlestown, Va, 2nd December, 1859

I John Brown am quite *certain* that the crimes of this *guilty, land: will* never be purged *away;* but with Blood. I had *as I now think: vainly* flattered myself that without *very much* bloodshed; it might be done.

John Brown rides atop his coffin on the way to his execution.

The gallows had been erected on the outskirts of town; Brown's final wagon ride was a short one. Along the way, Brown commented on the beautiful Virginia countryside through which he was passing. "This is beautiful country," he said. "I never had the pleasure of seeing it before." It was about eleven o'clock when the gallows came into view and the wagon came to a halt.

Hundreds of soldiers surrounded the gallows, ever vigilant for some last desperate attempt to rescue Brown and save his life. Brown, still dressed in the shabby clothes that he had worn on the night of the raid on Harpers Ferry, was ordered to step from the wagon and mount the scaffold. His hat was removed, and the noose was tightened around his neck. A white hood was placed over Brown's head, and he was ordered to step forward over the trapdoor in the scaffold.

John Brown ascends the scaffold to be hanged. On the way to the gallows, Brown commented on the scenery—seemingly unperturbed by his imminent death.

WITNESSES AT THE HANGING

The hanging of John Brown was witnessed by several hundred troops—Virginia militiamen, federal troops, cadets from the Virginia Military Institute—all summoned to service by Governor Henry Wise, who feared that Brown's supporters would stage some daredevil rescue attempt at the gallows minutes before the scheduled execution. Four of the soldiers watching the hanging would become famous in the troubling years to come.

Colonel Robert E. Lee commanded the federal troops in Charles Town. Less than two years after the hanging, at the start of the Civil War, he would be named commander of the Army of Northern Virginia of the Confederate States of America. Also in attendance was Professor Thomas Jackson of the Virginia Military Institute. Jackson would become Lee's second in command, earning the nickname "Stonewall" Jackson for his steadfastness on the battlefield. Lee and Jackson would fight side by side until the Battle of Chancellorsville in April 1863, where Jackson received a mortal wound.

Edmund Ruffin witnessed Brown's hanging and called Brown "a willing assistant, instead of the victim."

One of Jackson's cadets attending Brown's hanging was Edmund Ruffin. In the early morning of April 12, 1861, Ruffin would fire the first cannon blast toward the Union troops at Fort Sumter, the volley that marked the start of the Civil War. In his diary on the day of Brown's execution, Ruffin commented that Brown looked like "a willing assistant, instead of the victim."

Another eyewitness was a young soldier from the 1st Virginia Regiment of Richmond, an actor named John Wilkes Booth. Booth would leave the Confederate army before seeing combat in the Civil War; but on the evening of April 14, 1865, after all but a few of the Confederate armies had surrendered, Booth would fire the most damaging shot of the entire conflict, when he fired his pistol at the head of President Abraham Lincoln, who was enjoying a play at Ford's Theater in Washington. Lincoln died the next morning.

But then, at the moment of execution, there was a delay. Soldiers had to be moved into position. For ten minutes officers ordered their troops into formation, while Brown stood patiently, undoubtedly hoping that the hanging would finally be done. Finally, Brown reportedly mumbled, "Can't you be quick?"

With the troops in place, the sheriff, with an ax, cut the rope holding the trapdoor in place. Brown's body fell through the opening, the rope caught, and Brown's dead body dangled from the rope. An officer from the Virginia Military Institute shouted out, "So perish all such enemies of Virginia! All such enemies of the Union! All such foes of the human race!"

Doctors certified that Brown was dead. Brown's body was placed in its casket, and the black walnut box was readied for its journey north, to North Elba, Brown's family farm and final resting place.

The Burial

Brown's body was sent by train to Harpers Ferry, where Mary and a small group of her friends were ready to receive it. They spent the night at Wager House in Harpers Ferry, while Brown's coffin was kept under close guard. Before dawn the next day, the casket was loaded on a train for Philadelphia to begin the long journey to North Elba.

The mayor of Philadelphia was concerned that some individual might wish to do some damage to Brown's body when it reached his city. Philadelphia, located just north of the Mason-Dixon line, the imaginary border that separated the slave states from the free states, was the home of both abolitionists and proslavery people. To be certain that Brown's body would come to no harm, Brown's casket was secretly loaded onto a boat at a Delaware River crossing, while an empty wooden box, covered with a blanket, was delivered to the headquarters of the Philadelphia Anti-Slavery Society to pose as Brown's coffin.

Brown's body was taken by train from Camden, on the New Jersey side of the Delaware River, to New York City, where it was prepared for proper burial by a Manhattan undertaker. Brown's body was placed in a plain pine box, and the walnut casket was shipped back to Virginia. Brown would not be buried in a coffin made in a slave state. Mary Brown did not immediately make the trip to New York; she remained in Philadelphia with friends overnight, then departed by train for New York the next day.

From New York, Brown's casket was sent northward by train and wagon to North Elba. It arrived at the Brown family farm on December 7, and the burial was planned for the following day. Several prominent abolitionists had journeyed to North Elba to attend Brown's burial. Among them was Wendell Phillips, a fiery and eloquent orator and writer from Boston, and Reverend Joshua Young from Burlington, Vermont. On the evening before the burial, after supper Phillips delivered a two-hour eulogy of Brown to the friends and family members who had gathered at the Brown farmhouse.

The day of Brown's funeral was clear but very cold, near zero degrees. Neighbors labored hard to dig a grave into the frozen ground on the Brown farm. At one o'clock in the afternoon, a brief burial service commenced, with Reverend Young presiding and 250 friends, family members, and neighbors attending. Reverend Young read from one of the Epistles of Saint Paul, concluding with the words "I have fought the good fight; I have finished my course; I have kept the faith." Phillips spoke again, asserting, "Such a life was no failure. John Brown has loosed the roots of the slave system. . . . Virginia is weak because each man's heart has said 'amen' to John Brown." Then the members of the family of Lyman Epps, African American neighbors of the Browns, joined in the singing of "Blow Ye the Trumpets, Blow," Brown's favorite religious hymn:

> Blow ye the trumpets, blow
> Sweet is Thy work, my God, my King.
> I'll praise my Maker with my breath.
> O, happy is the man who hears.
> Why should we start, and fear to die.
> With songs and honors sounding loud.
> Ah, lovely appearance of death.

With that, John Brown's body was lowered into its grave and laid to rest.

LITERARY TRIBUTES

Soon after Brown's death, literary men and women began composing tributes to John Brown. Immediately after the execution, the abolitionist poet John Greenleaf Whittier penned the poem "Brown of Ossawatomie," which depicted a victorious Brown departing his jail cell on the way to his hanging and kissing the forehead of a slave child held by its mother (a scene that did not actually occur). Poet Walt Whitman, in "Year of Meteors," also commemorated the hanging of John Brown. On December 16, 1859, two weeks after Brown's death, a play titled *The Insurrection, or, Kansas and Harpers Ferry* opened at New York's Bowery Theatre. During the Civil War, Herman Melville, author of *Moby-Dick*, composed the poem "The Portent," which identified Brown as "the meteor of the war."

Brown continued to be the subject of many literary works after the Civil War and into the twentieth century. W. E. B. Du Bois, the great African American author and political leader, made Brown the subject of a 1909 biography. In 1928 the poet Stephen Vincent Benét composed perhaps the greatest literary work devoted to Brown, an epic poem titled *John Brown's Body*, which was awarded the year's Pulitzer Prize for poetry. In 1932 Leonard Ehrlich wrote a novel titled *God's Angry Man* that featured Brown as the protagonist. Ten years later Countee Cullen, the eloquent African American poet, commemorated Brown in the poem "A Negro Mother's Lullaby," which depicted an African American woman taking her child for a visit to Brown's grave. The poem describes Brown as living in heaven, "Close by the throne; / Tall he was living, / But now taller grown."

Brown continues to fascinate American writers. As recently as 1995, Brown was the subject of the novel *Raising Holy Hell* by Bruce Olds.

The Public Reaction

The public reaction to John Brown's hanging was, for the most part, predictable. Southerners saw the execution of Brown as just punishment for a sinful man. The *Daily Morning News* of Savannah, Georgia, condemned Brown as a "notorious horsethief, murderer, insurrectionist and traitor." Dozens of Southern newspapers and politicians echoed these sentiments.

Among abolitionists, Brown was, of course, deemed a hero, a saint, a martyr who had given his life for a just cause. But even Northerners who were not avid abolitionists were profoundly disturbed by the execution of John Brown. By facing his death with great courage and dignity, Brown had gained the sympathy of many Northerners who had not given much thought to the issue of slavery. Brown had converted many Americans to his cause, and he had at least earned the respect of thousands of others.

Hence, on the day of Brown's hanging, cities and towns throughout the North celebrated a special day of mourning. Church bells tolled. Banks and businesses closed, and citizens attended special prayer services at their churches. In auditoriums and town halls, politicians and orators delivered eulogies for Brown and issued strong condemnations of the slave system that Brown despised. In Boston, William Lloyd Garrison, who had earlier opposed Brown's use of violence to settle the slavery issue, defended Brown before a large crowd that had gathered at the Tremont Temple. "Yet, as a peace man—I am prepared to say: 'Success to every slave insurrection at the South, and in every slave country.' . . . Rather than see men wearing their chains in cowardly and servile spirit, I would, as an advocate of peace, much rather see them breaking the head of the tyrant with their chains."

On the day of Brown's execution, William Lloyd Garrison publicly defended Brown's use of violence while trying to abolish slavery.

Salutes and tributes poured out from literary men and women across the United States. Poets composed verses on Brown so that his name would live on. And about a year after Brown's death, at Northern church services and abolitionist meetings around the country, antislavery Americans began singing the words of a song called "John Brown's Body," which featured the words of some anonymous composer and the melody of a contemporary tune titled "Glory, Glory Hallelujah":

John Brown's body lies a-moulderin' in the grave,
John Brown's body lies a-moulderin' in the grave,
John Brown's body lies a-moulderin' in the grave,
But his soul is marching on!

John Brown was, indeed, dead and buried in December 1859. But he was not quickly forgotten.

Epilogue

His Soul Is Marching On!

JOHN BROWN WAS EXECUTED in Charles Town, Virginia, on December 2, 1859, and he was buried in North Elba, New York, several days later. That, however, was not the end of John Brown. His body had, indeed, been laid to rest, but his life, his spirit, his soul profoundly affected American history during the years following his death. Brown was unable to start a great slave rebellion at Harpers Ferry; instead the gunshots that he and his raiders fired there ignited a great civil war, the bloodiest chapter in American history. At the end of that war, Brown's goal would be achieved: The slaves would be free. And more than a century after that war, students of U.S. history and Americans fascinated by their nation's past continue to debate Brown's legacy.

The Coming of War

During the decade before Brown's death, the relationship between the Northern and Southern states had deteriorated to the point that both sides were preparing for civil war. The Compromise of 1850, designed to hold the Union together, only increased tensions between the North and South. In 1856 a limited civil war had broken out in Kansas over the issue of slavery. The Supreme Court's *Dred Scott* decision of 1857 angered the North, and Brown's raid convinced the South that it would soon be the target of a Northern invasion. Rumors flew that raids similar to Brown's were being planned all over the South, supported by Northern abolitionists.

Brown's Harpers Ferry raid marked an end to the time when peaceful compromise between the North and South was possible. In the halls of Congress, representatives from both regions now openly spoke of the coming crisis that would divide the Union and plunge the nation into a civil war. The situation in Washington was so tense that senators came to work armed for combat. "The members on both sides are mostly armed with deadly weapons, and it is said that the friends of each are armed in the galleries," wrote one senator to his wife. Another senator, commenting on the tense situation, stated, "The only men who don't have a revolver and a knife are those who have two revolvers." In a session of the House of Representatives on December 5, 1859, three days after Brown's execution, a Mississippi congressman charged Representative Thaddeus Stevens of Pennsylvania, an abolitionist, with a Bowie knife. A stabbing was averted when Stevens's Republican colleagues held back the knife-wielding Mississippian.

"Lawless Ruffians"

Two weeks after Brown's death, a Senate committee, chaired by Jefferson Davis of Mississippi, began a six-month investigation of the Harpers Ferry insurrection. The committee interviewed prominent Republicans and some of Brown's supporters but could not make a direct link between Brown and the Republican Party. The committee's report concluded that Brown's raid was "simply the act of lawless ruffians under the sanction of no public or political authority, against which Congress has no power to legislate."

But Southerners still privately believed that the Harpers Ferry affair was a first attempt by the North, and by the Republican Party in particular, to wage war to rid the South of its slaves. Brown's raid had united the South on that point. As the election of 1860 approached, many Southerners feared a Republican victory that would give the Republicans control of Congress and put a Republican in the White House. Then, reasoned the South's political leaders, their region would be politically powerless against the abolitionist North.

The election of Abraham Lincoln propelled the country further toward civil war.

In November 1860 Abraham Lincoln, the Republican candidate, was elected president. The South's worst fears became real. Lincoln, in his inaugural address, promised the suspicious South that his goals did not include abolishing slavery. Quoting from earlier speeches, Lincoln asserted, "I have no purpose, directly or indirectly, to interfere with the institution of slavery in the States where it exists." Southerners, however, pointed to a speech that Lincoln had made three years earlier in Springfield, Illinois, which became known as his "House Divided" speech:

"A house divided against itself cannot stand."

I believe this government cannot endure, permanently half *slave* and half *free*.

I do not expect the Union to be *dissolved*—I do not expect the house to *fall*—but I *do* expect it will cease to be divided.

It will become *all* one thing, or *all* the other.

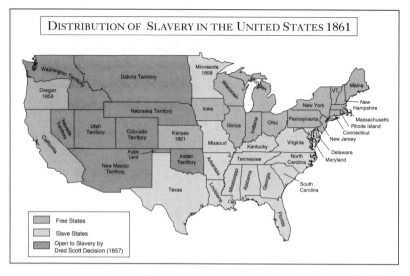

DISTRIBUTION OF SLAVERY IN THE UNITED STATES 1861

Free States

Slave States

Open to Slavery by
Dred Scott Decision (1857)

Soon after Lincoln's election, several Southern states fulfilled Lincoln's troubling prediction by seceding from the Union. Eventually eleven Southern states would withdraw and form the Confederate States of America. And on the morning of April 12, 1861, just a month after Lincoln took office as president, South Carolina troops began firing on Fort Sumter, a fortress in Charleston harbor held by federal troops. Thus, the Civil War began.

The next day Lincoln called for the enlistment of 75,000 federal troops to put down what he called the Southern rebellion. Many of those troops would sing "John Brown's Body" as their favorite marching song. But Lincoln would need more men than that. The Civil War lasted four years and, North and South, claimed the lives of more than 600,000 American soldiers.

Freeing the Slaves

The end of American slavery was the most important outcome of the Civil War. On January 1, 1863, President Lincoln implemented the Emancipation Proclamation. Lincoln referred to this executive order as "a fit and necessary war measure for suppressing said rebellion"; in it, he mandated that the slaves held in "the States and parts of States wherein the people thereof respectively, are this day in rebellion against the United States" are "and hence-forward shall be free."

Although Lincoln's original aim for the Civil War was to restore the Union, the fight quickly turned into a fight to abolish slavery. Many Union soldiers, like those pictured above, would sing "John Brown's Body" as they marched from battle to battle. After gaining their freedom at the end of the Civil War, many former slaves (left) still found themselves performing the back-breaking field work they had once been forced to do as slaves.

As the war came to an end, Congress proposed the Thirteenth Amendment to the Constitution. This amendment, which was ratified on December 18, 1865, several months after the conclusion of the Civil War, stated, "Neither slavery nor involuntary servitude, except as a punishment for crime whereof the party shall have been duly convicted, shall exist within the United States, or any place subject to their jurisdiction."

Slavery was not the only cause of the Civil War, but it was the main cause. Even Lincoln, who maintained that he was waging war not to end slavery but to hold together the Union, conceded in his Second Inaugural Address that slavery "constituted a peculiar and powerful interest. All knew that this interest was, somehow, the cause of the war."

John Brown was correct. American slavery would not be ended through political agitation, speeches, legislation, debate, compromise, or prayer. It would end only when blood was shed. Lincoln eventually concurred: God would not will the war to end until "the bond-man's two hundred and fifty years of unrequited toil shall be sunk, and until every drop of blood drawn with the lash, shall be paid by another drawn with the sword." John Brown drew the first blood of that war at Harpers Ferry, and after his trial, he became one of the war's early casualties.

Hero or Criminal?

Students of American history continue to debate the legacy of John Brown. Surely none today disagree with his basic premise: that slavery was an evil institution that needed to be eliminated from American society. But many Americans continue to question his methods. In a democratic society, where the people have the power to change the laws through peaceful, legal means, does an individual have the right to achieve his political goals by breaking the law, by stealing government property, by kidnapping government workers, by committing murder and arming others so that they might commit murder as well?

That is what John Brown did at Harpers Ferry; those are the crimes for which he was tried and executed. Although few Americans today would dispute the righteousness of his motive—to end slavery—should the people not condemn Brown as they condemn contemporary terrorists who attempt to achieve their goals by recklessly and violently breaking the law, by blowing up buildings or airplanes and taking the lives of innocent citizens? Many Americans today would undoubtedly agree with

Lincoln, who said that "although bad laws, if they exist, should be repealed as soon as possible, still while they continue in force, for the sake of example, they should be religiously observed."

On the other hand, many Americans looking back at John Brown and Harpers Ferry would likely agree with Henry David Thoreau, who argued that unjust laws should be broken, that Brown, after concluding that slavery could not be ended through peaceful means, had a right to use rifles to achieve his objective. In 1776 the colonial Founding Fathers had started a rebellion, had used cannon, musket, and sword, to free themselves from what they perceived to be the unjust rule of Great Britain. Was John Brown different from those who fought the American Revolution? John Anthony Copeland, one of Brown's raiders, thought not. In a letter to his brother, Copeland stated, "I am so soon to stand and suffer death for doing what George Washington, the so-called father of this great but slavery-cursed country, was made a hero for doing."

History might have proved Brown correct. Americans would eventually see slavery as he saw it, and, as Brown asserted, it would not be uprooted from American soil without substantial bloodshed. Perhaps Brown, by attempting to start a slave rebellion, was really trying to minimize that bloodshed, to ensure that the inevitable battle over slavery would be fought by the individuals directly affected by the institution: slaves and slaveholders. Instead, a four-year civil war that cost hundreds of thousands of lives was waged before slavery was eliminated from American life.

The debate on John Brown is not yet settled. It will continue as long as there are Americans who take an interest in their past, who find in the past compelling individuals and events that help explain present-day America.

Timeline

May 9, 1800
John Brown is born in Torrington, Connecticut. Five years later, the family would relocate to Ohio.

June 21, 1820
Brown marries Dianthe Lusk. The couple would have seven children before Dianthe's death in August 1832.

January 1, 1831
William Lloyd Garrison commences publication of the *Liberator,* the antislavery newspaper that would influence Brown and other abolitionists.

June 14, 1833
Brown marries Mary Day.

1850
The Compromise of 1850 attempts to relieve rising tensions between the North and South over the issue of slavery.

1854
The Kansas-Nebraska Act allows settlers in those two territories to determine by vote whether or not to allow slavery.

1855
Brown joins his sons in Kansas and participates in the civil war that was occurring in that territory over the issue of slavery.

1857
In the *Dred Scott* case, the Supreme Court rules that Congress cannot outlaw slavery in the U.S. territories.

1858
Brown forms the Secret Six, a group of abolitionists he would rely on for money and weapons with which to ignite a slave rebellion.

1859
Brown rents a farm in Maryland, several miles from Harpers Ferry, Virginia, site of the federal weapons arsenal. He plans to

capture the arsenal, arm the slaves of nearby farms and planta-tions, and ignite a slave rebellion that will consume the entire South.

October 16, 1859
Brown begins his raid on Harpers Ferry. Within thirty-six hours, he and most of his recruits are either killed or captured.

October 31, 1859
After a week-long trial in Charles Town, Virginia, followed closely in the newspapers by Americans across the nation, Brown is found guilty of murder and treason. On November 2, he is sentenced by Judge Richard Parker to hang.

December 2, 1859
Brown is hanged in Charles Town. His body is transported to North Elba, New York, and buried on the family farm on December 8.

November 1860
Abraham Lincoln, a Republican from Illinois, is elected presi-dent. During the subsequent months, eleven Southern states would withdraw from the Union.

April 12, 1861
The Civil War begins when South Carolina troops fire upon Fort Sumter, a garrison held by federal troops. The war lasts four years.

January 1, 1863
President Abraham Lincoln implements the Emancipation Proclamation, freeing the slaves in the states that had seceded from the Union.

December 18, 1865
The Thirteenth Amendment, outlawing slavery, becomes part of the Constitution.

For Further Reading

Stephen Vincent Benét, *John Brown's Body*. New York: Book-of-the-Month Club, 1980. This is an illustrated edition of Benét's 1928 epic poem, which contains detailed portraits of John Brown, Abraham Lincoln, and other key figures of the abolitionist movement and the Civil War.

Leonard Ehrlich, *God's Angry Man*. New York: Press of the Reader's Club, 1941. This 1932 novel features John Brown as its protagonist.

Doris Faber, *I Will Be Heard: The Life of William Lloyd Garrison*. New York: Lothrop, Lee and Shepard, 1970. This biography of Garrison was written for young-adult readers.

Stephen B. Oates, *Our Fiery Trial: Abraham Lincoln, John Brown, and the Civil War Era*. Amherst: University of Massachusetts Press, 1979. This history of the pre–Civil War era identifies John Brown's Harpers Ferry raid as the key event leading the United States into civil war.

Louis Ruchames, *A John Brown Reader*. London: Abelard-Schuman, 1959. This volume contains many of John Brown's letters and other written documents.

Martin Sleeper, *The Abolitionists: Protest in the Nineteenth Century*. Lexington, MA: Heath, 1970. This history of the abolitionist movement introduces readers to some of the era's key individuals.

Geoffrey C. Ward, Rick Burns, and Ken Burns, *The Civil War: An Illustrated History*. New York: Alfred A. Knopf, 1990. This history of the Civil War, based on the award-winning documentary film, takes readers, through text, illustrations, and interviews, from John Brown's raid through the end of the Civil War.

Works Consulted

Eric Foner and John A. Garrity, eds., *The Reader's Companion to American History*. Boston: Houghton Mifflin, 1991. This single-volume encyclopedia provides readers with information on the key events and individuals throughout American history.

Abraham Lincoln, *Selected Speeches and Writings*. New York: Vintage Books, 1989. This volume contains Lincoln's most important speeches and written texts.

Truman Nelson, *The Old Man at Harpers Ferry*. New York: Holt, Rinehart and Winston, 1973. This detailed history of John Brown's raid begins with the conspiracy and concludes with the burial.

Stephen B. Oates, *The Approaching Fury: Voices of the Storm, 1820–1861*. New York: HarperCollins, 1997. Using first-person narration, Oates allows thirteen key figures, including John Brown, to recount the events of the decade preceding the start of the Civil War.

————, *To Purge This Land with Blood: A Biography of John Brown*. New York: Harper & Row, 1970. Oates's study of John Brown is the most detailed accounting of his life available.

Benjamin Quarles, ed., *Blacks on John Brown*. Urbana: University of Illinois Press, 1972. This volume contains a century of commentaries on John Brown by African American writers.

Henry David Thoreau, *Civil Disobedience and Other Essays*. New York: Dover Publications, 1993. This volume contains several of Thoreau's most important essays, including "A Plea for Captain John Brown."

Index

Picture Credits

About the Author

James Tackach is the author of *Brown v. Board of Education* and young adult biographies of Roy Campanella, Henry Aaron, and James Baldwin. He has also authored *Historic Homes of America*, *Great American Hotels*, and *Fields of Summer: America's Great Ballparks and the Players Who Triumphed in Them*. His articles have appeared in the *New York Times*, the *Providence Journal, America's Civil War,* and a variety of academic publications. He teaches American literature at Roger Williams University in Bristol, Rhode Island, and lives in Narragansett, Rhode Island.